THE ANCIENT HISTORY OF THE "PALESTINIAN PEOPLE"

THE PALESTINIANS - THEIR ORIGIN, THEIR ROOTS, THEIR OBJECTIVE

I0407699

Tel: +97254-8030648

Email Address: kobimnsil@gmail.com

Website: www.kobisha.com

ABOUT THE AUTHOR

Kobi Shashoua is an author and a lecturer. Among his books you can find the most comprehensive book that exists to date about the Israeli-Palestinian conflict "Israel: the truth, the whole truth and nothing but the truth." This book leads the reader chapter by chapter through the complex reality of the conflict and dissects the causes for the crisis, uncovers to the reader the true faces of the parties involved, and presents the tactics, the strategies and the true objectives, that lie below the surface. The author also wrote the book series: "Facts you should know about the Middle East". The book you are holding in your hands is from that series.

The author, who resides in Israel, which is located in the most dangerous neighborhood of the world, in the heart of the Middle East, shares with us the facts together with the insights and the unique understanding of the region where he lives. We invite you to take part in this journey from a safe distance.

FOREWORD

There is no one who doesn't know the Palestinians or heard about them. Their share in global population is negligible, yet the amount of references is not less than that of the great powers. In fact, a positive reference of the Palestinians is usually accompanied by a negative reference of the State of Israel, the conquering power. Moreover, the establishment of the State of Israel on May 14th 1948 marks also the inception of the Palestinian refugee problem, a problem that has been dragging on for over 60 years. World War II has created huge waves of refugees. These refugees have eventually found a place of refuge. But only one refugee issue continues to resonate. Why? The answer for that, later on. Are the Palestinians really who they claim to be? Is there really a solution to the refugee problem? Will there be peace between the Palestinians and the Israelis – the Jews? The answers to these questions and to other questions I will present in this book.

Table of Contents

Genesis

In every excavation around the region, thousands of archaeological evidences indicating the existence of a Jewish settlement thousands of years before the Prophet Mohammed was born can be found (by the way, the State of Israel has no control over the subject matter taught and transmitted in the Palestinian Authority that has been laboring for years to blur and to conceal the connection between the Jewish people and the Land of Israel).

The presence of archaeological remains throughout the Land of Israel, indicate a connection of over 3,000 years between the Jewish people and its land, an argument that is difficult to contend with. Therefore, the Palestinian Authority is making sure to blur this connection and to bury the evidences under a veil of lies and to invent an ancient connection between the "Palestinian" people and their stolen homeland.

"Only in Palestine....after 60 years of excavations, and they (the Zionist) failed. Not a jug of water, not even a single coin, no clay tools, no bronze weapons, not a piece of metal, nothing from the myth because it is a lie. The excavations have been thoroughly examined and nevertheless they didn't uncover any archaeological findings". [1] This is what thousands of

---

(1) A lecture by Dr. Jamal Amar at the Bir-Zeit Palestinian University located in the Bir-Zeit village north of Ramallah in the West Bank.
http//www.palwatch.org/main.aspx?fi=487

Palestinians are taught, but I ask the same question only in the context of the "Palestinian people", where are the archaeological proofs of the existence of this ancient people?

WANTED

Artifacts from "Palestinians Civilization"

$100,000,000
REWARD

The question naturally arises, from where did the name Palestine come to this area, what is the region called Palestine and who are these people named after it.

So who are the Palestinians?

Before we answer this let's check one more thing: just as it is indisputable that E=MC [2], thus it is indisputable that P=B. In Arabic, the letter "P" is preannounced like the letter "B". [2]

You tell me, how can there be a nation that is unable to pronounce its name?

MAKES NO SENSE!

---

[2] The Arabic language lacks the ability to pronounce the letter "P". Any attempt to pronounce the letter "P" sounds unequivocally like the letter "B".

Just as the British and the Americans are unable to pronounce the letter "CH" or guttural consonants due to language barrier, the Arabs are unable to pronounce the letter "P" and it comes out like "B". In fact, if you ask a "Palestinian" in the street to pronounce the word "Palestine" he will pronounce it "Falastine" or "Balastine". How can people exist that are unable to pronounce their name? Don't try to ask this from those "Palestinians" who appear in the media and attack the State of Israel in fluent English and tell heaps of lies about it. They are well trained in the secrets of the English language and the international language. If you ask an ordinary citizen, he will tell you proudly that he is a proud "Falastinian".

Why should you believe me – after all, you hear all the time the words "Free Palestine", "We are the Palestinians", "I'm Palestinian", and here I come and argue that in fact the Palestinians cannot pronounce their name and instead it comes out "Balestinian". The fact is that there is a difficulty to pronounce the letter "P" in the Arabic language, which sounds instead as the letter "B". I will present to you a short passage from a trial conducted in the United States that dealt with some confusion caused when an Arab tourist arrived in the United States and was asked to explain what the strange object in his suitcase was. You are welcome to read the article. It is not relevant to the book except for understanding that the communication failure was caused by the inability to pronounce the letter "P". This is the relevant part from the article:

"The attorney added that XXX, an Iraqi, has a thick accent and she herself had trouble understanding him….She said she recently learned Arabic speakers sometimes have trouble distinguishing "P" and "B" sounds." [3]

---

[3] http://www.nbcnews.com/id/14836453#.UUf_IBeeNr0

You understand, Palestine is not an Arab name but a name that originates in the Greek and in the Latin languages. Thus, it contains elements from the Greek and the Latin languages that do not exist in Arabic, such as the letter "P". Therefore, the Palestinians cannot pronounce it and instead it sounds "Balestinians", or the more common name "Falastine".

In history (the real one, not the rewritten one), there was indeed an ancient people who lived in the region and was called: The Philistine people. The philistines were sailors, and their ethnic origin (according to archeological findings) was the Mycenaean Greek culture. The Philistines settled in the southern coastal region of Canaan. Their domicile was called "Peleset". [4]

---

[4] From Wikipedia under the entry: "Philistines".

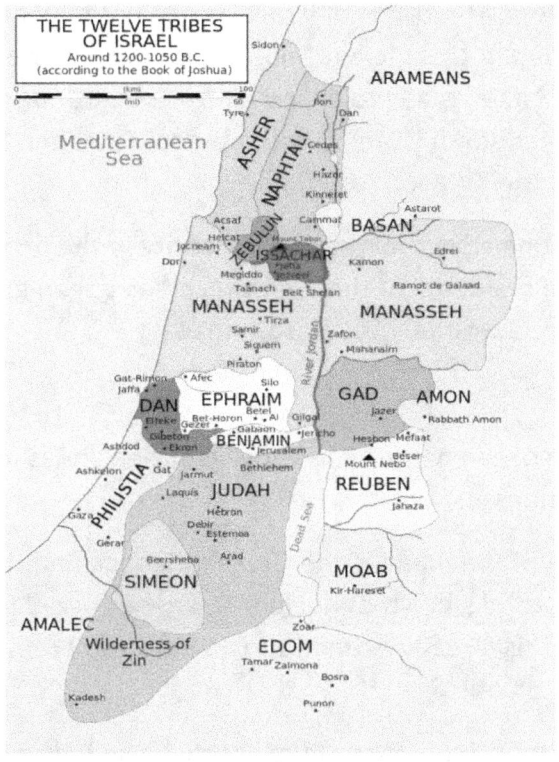

Before we continue, let's check what Canaan is:

Canaan is an ancient term referring to the area that includes Israel, Lebanon, the Palestinian Authority, parts of Jordan, Syria and northern eastern parts of Egypt.

This map is dated to the 12th century before the birth of Jesus and about 1,800 years before the birth of the Prophet Mohammad. Please note the names of the tribes. These are the 12 tribes of Israel. To this day the name Judah has been kept, but as part of that deliberate blurring, the name Judah is slowly replaced by the words "The West Bank".

---

[5] From Wikipedia under the entry: "The tribes of Israel".

I will explain briefly who the 12 tribes that ruled the land of Canaan were. The tribes of Israel were a national entity and an ethnic group in the ancient Middle East, who made up the people of Israel as a whole, and who were later untied as the United Kingdom of Israel. It was later split into the Kingdom of Israel and the Kingdom of Judah. [5]

The philistines lost their national identity in the 5th century BC. The mixed residents of the Philistine cities began gradually to convert to Judaism by the Hasmonean. [6]

Remember:

The origin of the name "Palestine" is Greek and is named after the Philistines.

The origin of the name is the Greek language and the Latin languages, and since that ancient European people "the Philistines" is already extinct, the question still remains: who are the "Palestinians"?

Before we continue, let us take a walk again in the mysteries of history, in order to understand the origin of the name "Palestine", the name that the Palestinians and their Muslim allies are waving all over the world.

This region has been conquered by many empires. The first conquest after AD was of the Roman Empire. The Roman period in the Land of Israel starts in the year 63 BC with the conquest by Pompey, until the year 324 AD, a period that is generally considered as the beginning of the rule of the Byzantine Empire.

---

[6] A family of Jewish priests and fighters in the Kingdom of Judea during the Second Temple (in the first and second centuries BC)

During this period the name "Palestine" was coined to the Land of Israel. Following the rebellion of Simon bar Kokhba ,[7] an attempt was made by Hadrian to impose on the Jews decrees that were aimed to destroy their cultural and national unity and to uproot the Jewish religion from the Land of Israel, and thus to liquidate the resistance to Roman rule. The Roman Emperor Hadrian [8] changed the name of the province from Judea to "Syria Palestina", named after the extinct Philistine people. [9]

---

[7] The Bar Kokhba uprising was a rebellion of the Jews in the Land of Israel against the rule of the Roman Empire under the Emperor Hadrian, in the years 132-136 AD. At the head of the uprising was Simon Bar Kokhba who had the support of the scholars of his generation led by Rabbi Akiva. Initially the uprising was successful, but later on it was brutally suppressed. Hundreds of thousands of Jews were killed and the Jewish community in the Land of Israel was almost extinct. The three years in which Bar Kokhba ruled in Judea were the last period of independence of the Jewish people in their homeland, until the establishment of the State of Israel.   From Wikipedia under the entry: "Bar Kokhba uprising"

[8] Hadrian, (24th January 76 – 10th July 138), was emperor of Rome from the year 117 until his   death. He is regarded as the third of the Five Good Emperors, and the period of his rule is considered one of the more prosperous during the reign of the Emperors. On the other hand, in Jewish tradition he is known as a very negative figure due to the suppression of the Bar Kokhba uprising when hundreds of thousands Jews were killed, including the ten martyrs, and his religious persecutions known as the Hadrian persecutions.
From Wikipedia under the entry: "Hadrian".

[9] From Wikipedia under the entry: "The Roman period in the Land of Israel".

Let us move forward. Today there is a "Palestinian people". No one denies that. But since there is no historical evidence or archeological remains, it is advisable to check when and from where it popped up.

We will move on to the modern history of the 20th century.

The period of the British Mandate 1920-1948: [10]

Four hundred years of Ottoman rule in the Land of Israel came to an end when it surrendered to the British on December 9th, 1917. The surrender was affirmed by the British general Edmund Allenby and the previous rule was replaced by a British martial law.

The League of Nations was founded after World War I (1914-1918). The League of Nation passed a resolution that nations that were not sufficiently developed to maintain an independent government will accept the rule of more developed nations until they reach self-maturity.

The validity of this decision was reflected in Article 22 of the League of Nations Covenant, which was signed at the Paris Convention in 1919, and was given a practical expression in the Treaty of Versailles [11] which was signed on July 28th, 1919.

The implementation of the various articles of the Treaty was discussed by the representatives of the Powers in the "San Remo conference" in April 1920. The territories occupied during World War I were divided between the Powers.

---

[10] From Wikipedia under the entry: "The British Mandate".

[11] The Treaty of Versailles was signed after the defeat of Germany in World War I. Germany signed the treaty and the wording was according to the various interests of the Entente (The Allies): The United States, France, Britain and Italy.

Britain was assigned to implement the Balfour Declaration [12], a document signed by the British Foreign Secretary, Lord Arthur James Balfour, on November 2nd 1917, which dealt in essence with the establishment in the Land of Israel of a national home for the Jewish people.

The declaration, orchestrated by Dr. Chaim Weizmann and with the cooperation of the British Zionist leadership, was delivered to Lord Walter Rothschild and included the recognition in the rights of the Jewish people to their historic land and the rights of the Jews to immigrate to it. The British cabinet endorsed the version of the Declaration on October 31st 1917.

At that time a "Palestinian people" was not formed yet. In fact, it was formed in 1967, but let's progress a few lines further on the toolbar of history.

Let us see what the Arab inhabitants of Palestine thought at that time.

The first Congress of the Muslim-Christian organizations was held in Jerusalem in February 1919. The conference was convened in order to elect an Arab representative to the peace talks held in Paris. The decision made at the Congress by the representatives was that Palestine is an integral part of Syria (Greater Syria) and has never been separated from it. The connection with Syria is tied with thick ropes by religion, by nationality, by language, by economy and by the geography of the region. [13]

---

[12] From Wikipedia under the entry: "The Belfour Declaration".

[13] Wikipedia under the entry: "Palestinian people".

Please remember the term "Greater Syria". This term will be relevant when we get to the reasons that led to the formation of the "Palestinian people".

During his visit to the region in 1867, the author Mark Twain described the land, the promised land, in the following way: "....these desserts are empty, unpopulated, these faded mounds of wasteland....take this heap of ruins, Kfar Nahum; take Tiberias, a silly village dozing off in the shadow of its six dilapidated palm trees; that deserted hillside where the swine of the Miracle of the Swine raced into the sea and thought, undoubtedly, that they had better swallow demons and ghosts and even drown in the water, than to carry on living in such a place...take this monotonous, dreary, sailing free lake, and put it in a ring of yellow hills and low and steep banks...all these things – if they are not an excellent material for a lullaby that puts you to sleep, then there can be no lullaby in the world". [14]

This region was sparsely populated.

11 years earlier, a book was published in London, titled "Sinai and Palestine". The book was published in 1856 and was written by Arthur Penrhyn Stanley. Stanley was Dean of Westminster and a theologian (a philosopher and a clergyman) in Oxford. From the winter of 1852 until the spring of 1853, Arthur with three of his friends toured Egypt, Palestine (Israel), Lebanon and Syria.

---

[14] Wikipedia under the entry: "A pleasure trip to the Holy Land" (Mark Twain, "A pleasure trip to the Holy Land", Ariel publishing, Jerusalem 1999).

With the help of his friends from Oxford, Stanley edited his impressions of the region in a 530 pages book. [15]

On page 120 he writes:

"And this brings us to the question which Eastern travelers so often ask, and are asked, on their return, can these stony hills, these deserted valleys, be indeed the Land of Promise, the Land flowing with milk and honey?"

The testimony of these two authors does not leave any doubt that this was desert land, desolate, barren and with stony ground.

The sharp- eyed ones may say, so what is the point? That there were no Palestinians at that time and therefore they cannot bring claims for stealing their homeland? But the same thing is valid also regarding the Jews. After all, if this region was indeed desolate, then it is reasonable that the Jewish population as well was scarce. I can only agree. But that is not the point.

Stop and think for a moment. If this region was indeed desolate, from where did the millions of Palestinians who are now claiming the "right of return" emerge, the right to return to their stolen homeland? But only a little less than 150 years ago, an American author and a British author have found, 11 years apart, the country desolate. And if so, where from did a nation spring up that claims to have thicker historical roots in the land than those of the Jews.

---

[15] The book can be found in the digital library of Google under:
http://books.google.co.il/books?id=IfhAAAAAcAAJ&printsec=frontcover&dq=sina i+and+palestine+by+arthur&source=bl&ots=7ZVVilGPON&sig=eSKxP5ynejc7Sm2n 7cSRGuX0kSY&hl=iw&ei=VYeYTJ26AYiPswbBr8iVDA&sa=X&oi=book_result&ct=re sult&resnum=7&ved=0CCoQ6AEwBg#v=onepage&q&f=false

Day and night the Palestinian spread the argument that the origin of the Jews in the State of Israel is their immigration from Europe. The origin of part of this immigration is the Arab countries that expelled their Jews and turned them into refugees (more about this in the chapter that deals with the subject of the eternal refugee problem). The Palestinians argue incessantly that the Jews have no holding in this place since they are "immigrants sponsored by imperialism" [16] that ruled here.

Until the establishment of the State of Israel in 1948, the British ruled this region under the Mandate. The entire region was called "Palestine", a name borrowed from the Roman conqueror who gave the region that name (Palestine), in 63 AD. During the Mandate all the inhabitants in this region were called Palestinians – Jews, Muslims, Christians etc. After the end of the British Mandate and the establishment of the State of Israel in 1948, the inhabitants living in the new country were called Israelis.

---

[16] A reminder: imperialism is the takeover of countries and people by one country and the utilization of their resources to increase the power and the wealth of the imperialistic country.

Please note that the coin is dated 1942, about 6 years before the Declaration of Independence of the State of Israel. The name "Palestine" appears on the coin in bold letters in 3 languages: Arabic, English and Hebrew. Palestine meaning the entire region of the Land of Israel and its inhabitants whether they are Arabs or Jews they are all called Palestinians. Pay attention that in the Hebrew writing of the name "Palestine" the initials of the Hebrew name Land of Israel appear in brackets in bold letters.

The bank responsible for issuing the note is the Anglo-Palestine Bank Ltd. (The National Bank as from 1951). This is a of one Palestinian pound bill, in English "ONE PALESTINE POUND". In Hebrew: one Israeli Lira.

Photo: Arkady Mazor / Shutterstock.

This is a stamp from that period. In the background is the Tower of David in Old Jerusalem. Here as well the name Palestine appears in 3 languages: English, Arabic and Hebrew, which indicates the composition of the population at that time that included Jewish Palestinians, Arab Palestinians and the British who ruled the region under the Mandate they received from the League of Nations.

The refusal of the Arab countries to accept the U.N. Partition Plan, that recommended to establish in this region a Home for the Jewish people and also an Arab country, led to the outbreak of the War of Independence. On May 14th 1948, with the end of the British Mandate and the declaration of the establishment of the State of Israel, the armies of Egypt, Jordan, Iraq, Syria and Lebanon invaded the country. At the end of the war, ceasefire agreements were signed with four countries: Egypt, Syria, Jordan and Lebanon.

The borders of Israel were specified in the agreements (only part of Jerusalem was included in the State of Israel), the West Bank [17] was annexed to the Kingdom of Jordan and the Gaza Strip was annexed to Egypt.

When the Arab countries realized that it was difficult to bring about the destruction of the State of Israel, they decided to set up the "Palestine Liberation Organization" (PLO). Thus the organization was founded on June 2nd 1964, headed by Ahmad Shukeiri.

In his speech at the Security Council in May 31th 1956, Shukeiri said: "The general opinion is that Palestine is an integral part of southern Syria". [18]

Ahmed Shukeiri, Head of the Palestine Liberation Organization, was born in 1908 in Lebanon. His father's Arab family immigrated to Egypt from the Hejaz (a region in the west of Saudi Arabia) and his mother was Turkish. He cannot be called a Palestinian, yet he was Head of the "Palestine Liberation Organization". His duties included, among other things: Member of the Syrian delegation to the United Nations (1949-1951), Assistant to the Secretary of the Arab League (1950-1956), Saudi Arabia's ambassador to the United Nations (1957-1962), and the Chairman of the PLO [19] (1964-1967).

The various functions of Shukeiri were not written without a purpose. The Arabs see themselves as one nation, and this has enabled him to serve both as a Member of the Syrian delegation, and as Saudi Arabia's ambassador, and as the Chairman of the PLO and the assistant to the Secretary of the Arab League.

---

[17] An emphasis on how the real name was buried under the narrative of the "West Bank".

[18] http://www.palestinefacts.org/pf_1948to1967_plo_backgd.php

[19] Palestine Liberation Organization.

But nothing will change the historical reality – Ahmed Shukeiri was not a Palestinian! Moreover, even though he was appointed to Head the Palestine Liberation Organization, a few years earlier he said that Palestine was a part of Syria.

Years later, the Nobel Peace Prize laureate Yasser Arafat, was appointed to lead the organization. This is the name most of us are familiar with and some of us even associate it with him being the leader of the PLO. In an interview with the Italian reporter Ariana Plazi in 1970, he said that "the issue of the borders does not interest us...from an Arab point of view we must not talk about borders. Palestine is a drop in the ocean of the Arab nation stretching from the Atlantic Ocean to the Red Sea and beyond...the PLO fights Israel in the name of Pan-Arabism. The place you call "Jordan" is just more of Palestine". [20]

And he knew what he was talking about.

At first the British Mandate included the entire area of Jordan and of the State of Israel. In 1922, according to the decision made by Winston Churchill, the British Secretary of State for the Colonies, the Trans Jordan areas were administratively separated from Western Israel, called Palestine. Note, in fact a British Minister decided to call the region Palestine. On May 14th 1923, with the approval of the League of Nations Council, the British were authorized to administrate Trans Jordan not for the implementation of the Balfour Declaration. Thus Britain granted autonomy to Eastern Trans Jordan with the leadership of the Emir Abdullah. [21]

---

[20] http://www.freerepublic.com/focus/f-news/2201793/posts

[21] For further details see Wikipedia under the entry: "The British mandate".

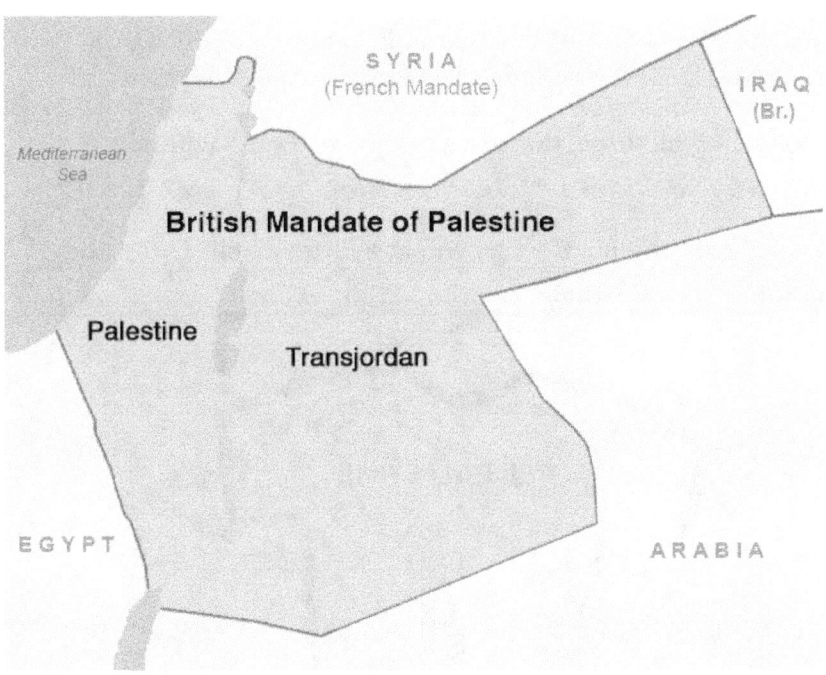

From Wikipedia under the title: "The British Mandate".
creator: Zero0000

The illustration shows the entire area that was destined initially to constitute a National Home for the Jews including the area east of the Jordan River. The withdrawal from the Balfour Declaration to which the British were committed started gradually under the pressure of the Arabs, and what was eventually left from the promise were bits of land from the total area.

Jordan got its name, eventually, not due to the presence of some ancient people named "Jordan", but because the Jordan River crossed the region. Eastern Trans Jordan is called "Jordan" and that is the name adopted by the inhabitants of the area. The western side of Jordan is called "Palestine". In fact, the British restored the Greek name to the area.

If it has already been decided to form a people out of nothing, and I am talking about the "Palestinian" people, it`s only right to invent for them a flag with motifs and symbols of independence. And now to the riddle:

In the following pictures, there are two flags. Could you find differences between the pictures?

Those who solve the puzzle may win in a lottery a shirt with the inscription "Free Palestine":

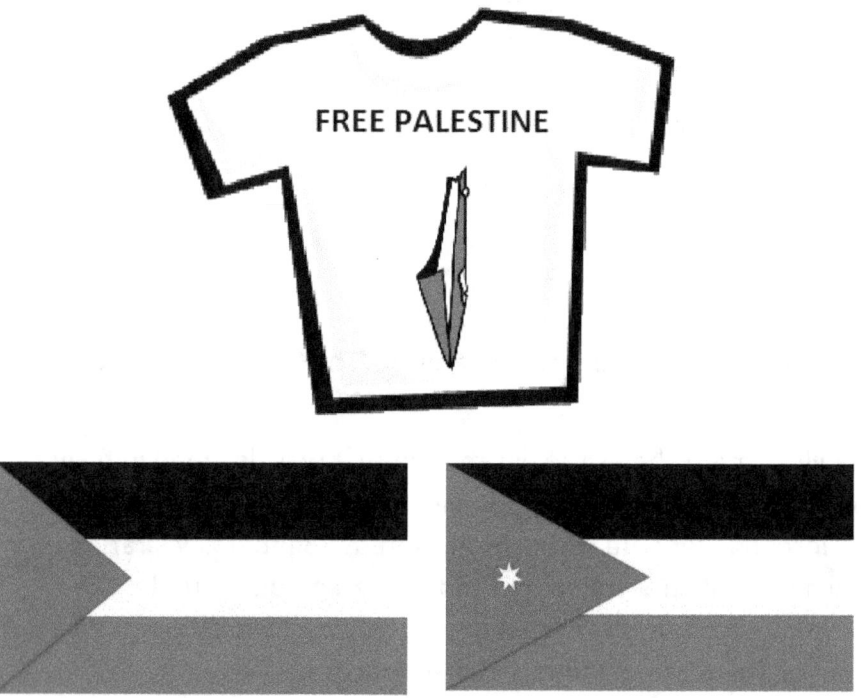

The flag on the right is a Jordanian flag. The flag on the left – is the flag of "Palestine". The main obvious difference is the absence of the star from the Palestinian flag. Other than that, I would say that the copy is quite identical to the original. In university, it would be considered plagiarism.

NO CHEATING!

So what were the objectives of the organization headed by Arafat? Was it to guarantee the Palestinians a state? Or maybe to liberate this region from the yoke of the infidel in order to achieve the objective of all Arabs wherever they are? Thinks about it!

The objective of the Palestine Liberation Organization had no connection whatsoever to the Palestinian people and its vision. The real objective was to destroy the State of Israel and to enable the pan-Arabic vision come true.

What Arafat and Ahmed Shukeiri tried to materialize, Zouheir Mohsen expressed well openly.

Zouheir Mohsen (1936-1979) served as Secretary General of the al-Saika (1971-1979), a Palestinian organization that operated in Syria and was a part of the PLO. [22]

Here is what Zuheir Mohsen had to say about the "Palestinian people" in an interview with the Dutch newspaper "Trouw" in March 1977: "A Palestinian people does not exist.

---

[22] From Wikipedia under the entry: "Zuheir Mohsen"

[23] The photo was taken from the Arabic Wikipedia under the entry: "Map of Palestine", where the role of Israel in the Middle East is explained: "The Zionists are the reason for instability, for war and destruction in the Middle East. The only solution for securing stability in the Middle East is to bring to an end the rule of the thieves and the terrorists and the return of Palestine to the Palestinians". Tell it to the tens of thousands of Muslims slaughtered in Syria, Yemen, Lebanon, Egypt, Libya, Tunisia etc, uninterruptedly.

The creation of a Palestinian state is only as a means for continuing our struggle against the State of Israel, for our Arab unity. In today's reality, there is no difference between Jordanians, Palestinians, Syrians, and Lebanese.

It is only for political and tactical purposes that we speak today about the existence of a "Palestinian people", since Arab national interests necessitate the existence of a "Palestinian people" as opposition to Zionism….for tactical purposes, Jordan, which is a sovereign state with defined borders, cannot claim Haifa or Jaffa, while as a Palestinian, I can undoubtedly claim Haifa, Jaffa, Beer-Sheba and Jerusalem. However, the moment we get a foothold in all Palestine, we will not wait even one minute to unite Palestine and Jordan".

Did you understand?

To be fair, I should point out that not everybody endorses this trick. There are some decent people who did not agree with this idea.

During a meeting with PLO leaders in 1976, the Syrian President Hafez al-Assad referred to Palestine as part of southern Syria. He turned to the Palestinian delegates and said "You do not represent Palestine more than us. Do not forget one thing: there is no 'Palestinian people', there is no Palestinian identity there is only Syria! You are an integral part of the Syrian people and Palestine is an integral part of Syria. Therefore we, the Syrian authorities, are the true representatives of the Palestinian people". [24]

I mentioned previously the expression "Greater Syria". That is the meaning. The area called Palestine, as well, is an area that Syria considers as a part of it.

---

[24] http://www.danielpipes.org.174/palestine-for-the-syrians

When the Syrian President talks about Palestine he refers to the entire region that encompasses today the State of Israel, the Palestinian Authority and the Gaza Strip. No one was talking about a Palestinian state alongside an Israeli state. All of them spoke about a Palestinian state over the entire Area and that is what they are talking about today as well!

The former Arab Member of the Knesset Azmi Bishara, who escaped from Israel after being accused of passing on information to the enemy in wartime, was interviewed in a talk show where he claimed that "There is no such thing as "Palestinian people", it is a fabrication – there is an Arab nation!" [25]

On the other hand, it is impossible to deny the existence of the "Palestinian people", it is alive and kicking. In historical perspective, the existence of the "Palestinian people" is a fait accompli. Undoubtedly that after three generations that have been educated as a people, the younger generation has no doubt about its Palestinian identity. As far as the younger generation is concerned it is indisputable that its country was stolen by the "Zionist enemy". But its roots stem from in a big lie that created it as a separate entity during the 60's, as another way of fighting against the State of Israel.

I hope that eventually the wish of the "Palestinian people" to have a country will be stronger than the wishful thinking of its senders to wipe out the State of Israel, as it happened to Australia that was, originally, a penal colony of the British Empire and became an independent state.

---

[25] http://www.youtube.com/watch?v=U1KkYjhFryA

As time passes, the primary objectives wear out in the face of the actual facts. I hope the "Palestinian people" gets a country of its own located next to the borders of the State of Israel. I hope, but am aware of it that at present, due to the education the "Palestinian people" gets from its leaders and from its senders, the current generation is quite lost. I wish I am wrong – I will be happy to be wrong!

I hope you understand the truth regarding the big lie called the "Palestinian people", particularly after its authentic representatives have exposed by mere words the big lie and its objective. Nevertheless, a "Palestinian people" exists today, numbering over 11 million Palestinians. [26]

The question is, where from did the numbers swell and reach the number of 11 million Palestinians, similar to the number of the Jewish people that exists already for thousands of years?

As we have seen, the founding father of this people, Ahmed Shukeiri, was not a Palestinian at all but a Lebanese. Since the Palestinians were invented, then anyone can be a Palestinian.

In addition, the high birth rate of about 5 children per family [27] is also an effective demographic weapon, as was well expressed by Yasser Arafat: "The womb of an Arab woman is my strongest weapon"... and you have a people that grows in a geometrical progression.

---

[26] From Wikipedia under the entry: "Palestinian people"

[27] From UNICEF, Http://www.unicef.org/infobycountry/oPt_statistics.html

With the formation of the "Palestinian people" the tables have turned. From a situation in which a tiny Jewish country is threatened by the Arab nation numbering 22 countries the area of which is much larger than that of Europe, the State of Israel has become the country that is threatening a weak people dispossessed of its land.

Something to think about – notice how the use of children produces a violation of balance. And they know it very well, so that the use of children has become a central motif in every discourse, demonstration and presentation. Remember what Golda Meir, the Israeli Prime Minister, expressed so well in the words: "We could forgive the Arabs for killing our children, but we could not forgive them for forcing us to kill their children. Peace with the Arabs will prevail when they will love their children more than they hate us. "

Palestinian boys throw stones at Israeli tanks stationed close to the headquarters of the Palestinian leader Yasser Arafat in the West Bank town of Ramallah, 07 February 2002. Arafat has been under virtual house arrest by Israel since 03 December 2001.
AFP PHOTO/Jamal Aruri

The thought today is that the solution to the conflict is the restoration of the rights stolen from the Palestinians by the "Zionist conqueror", and then finally peace and quiet will reach the region. At the time when the "Palestinian people" was invented, this saying would have aroused a rolling laughter.

But today, a few generations later, there may be truth in that in terms of "the cocoon rises against its maker". Two Arab countries have signed a peace agreement (very cold) with Israel, a few Arab countries have become neutral and the conflict is with the "Palestinian" people that wishes to fulfill its right to a country of its own 2-3 generations after its invention. The young people born in recent years to Palestinian parents were born into a coherent perception of a "Palestinian people", and the voice of the young people is more important than the voice of its spokesmen.

Those spokesmen talk about wiping out the State of Israel and establishing a Palestinian state on all the territory of Palestine under the British Mandate. The aspiration of the young people for a country is a positive aspiration! But let us hope that the aspirations are for a Two-States solution, and not for one Palestinian state that in essence wishes: "The Jewish men to the sea, and the women for us". [28]

In the next chapter we will discuss the issue of the Palestinian refugees. Millions of Palestinian refugees are waiting to return to the "land of their forefathers". Let's learn about them.

---

[28] This expression was used by Ahmed Shukeiri to excite and to inflame the blood-thirsty masses. If there are no 72 virgins around, at least we will unburden the stored sexual fury one Jewish women, after we butcher the men of course!

The eternal refugee problem

"There will be no peace without a solution to the Palestinian refugee problem", "We will not give up the right of return", "The refugee problem must be resolved". It is very likely that whoever watches the news from time to time comes cross one of the versions of these statements. The Palestinian refugee problem is so serious, that the UN appointed a special agency dedicated exclusively to dealing with it. It turns out that the Palestinian refugee situation is so awful that the rest of the 32 million refugees around the world are neglected in sub-committees of the UN [29]. The millions of refugees from the recent wars in Africa, from the flaming Middle East and from the third world countries, and even refugees as a result of natural disasters, are   forgotten in the corridors of the UN. Why? Because the Palestinian refugee problem is the most important one.

But, what is a refugee?

The UN founded a Refugee Agency known as The UN Office of The High Commissioner for Refugees (UNHCR).

The UN High Commissioner for Refugees (the UNHCR) is a UN organization that acts to protect and support refugees and asylum seekers worldwide, by taking care that the agreements in the UN Convention Relating to the Status of Refugees are implemented.

The UN Convention Relating to the Status of Refugees: the International Convention on the Status of the Refugees was signed in 1951 in order to ensure protection to people who were forced to escape from their country in order to save their lives.

---

[29] http://www.unhcr.org/4a2fd52412d.html.

These people are defined as refugees and the Convention formulates a set of human rights to which these refugees are entitled.

The definition of a refugee in the Convention: a refugee is a person who escaped or who was expatriated from his country or from his permanent home, due to a well-founded fear of being persecuted for reasons of race, religion, nationality or political opinion. [30]

In addition, the Convention defines what people are excluded from the definition "refugee": war criminals, a person who has committed a crime against humanity or any other non-political serious crime.

This Agency deals with all the refugees in the world, except for Palestinians, who have their own Agency called UNRWA! The UNRWA (The United Nations Relief and Works Agency for Palestine Refugees in the Near East) provides support and protection to about 5 million Palestinian refugees registered in Jordan, Lebanon, Syria, and in the "Palestinian occupied territories". [31]

Why is it that in the UN there are two organizations whose function is to handle refugees? Why is it that one organization allocates resources only for handling the Palestinian refugee problem and another organization deals with all the rest? How is the status of a Palestinian refugee different from that of any other refugee on the planet?

---

[30] http//www.unhcr.org/pages/49c3646c125.html

[31] http://www.unrwa.org/htemplate.php?id=87

A phrase I heard once: "All people are equal, but some are more equal". It seems that this law applies here.

And now a riddle:

There are 9,700 employees at the UN Office of The High Commissioner for Refugees (UNHCR) who handle around 96 million refugees (regular refugees, not the Palestinians). [32]

UNRWA – The UN Nations Relief and Works Agency for Palestine Refugees in the Near East provides support, protection and advocacy to about 5 million Palestinian refugees.

And now the question:

How many people are employed by UNRWA?

1. A simple and logical calculation: if for 96 million refugees 9,700 workers are employed, then for around 5 million Palestinian refugees less than 5 percent are supposed to be employed, namely about 500 employees.
2. Yet it is a separate Agency, so in a proper exaggeration, I would argue that about 5,000 people are employed by it.
3. Let us go wild and assert 12,000 employees.
4. No answer is correct.

Answer number 4 is correct. Since the real answer is 30,000 members of staff. [33] (As of 2016)

MAKES NO SENSE!

---

[32] http://www.unhcr.org/figures-at-a-glance.html

[33] http://www.unrwa.org/who-we-are/organizational-structure

Namely, if for all the 9,896 refugees and those who seek asylum there is one staff member from the UNHCR, then for every 167 Palestinian refugees there is one staff member. The ratio is almost 1 to 59 in favor of the Palestinians.

I repeat: for the same amount of refugees, the Palestinians get personnel almost 59 times larger than the rest of the refugees around the world.

Perhaps it is appropriate to add that 99% of the UNRWA employees are Palestinians.   Thus, from a short-term committee that was established in order to deal with the issue of the Palestinian refugees after the War of Independence in 1948, the numbers have grown more and more, and the committee has turned into an eternal organization, the objective of which is   never to resolve the Palestinian refugee problem. Merely the pension fund of the Agency`s employees has passed the one billion dollars threshold. [34] If so, why really not to continue with it forever?

In February 2009 a report was published in which the former Attorney General of the Relief Agency UNRWA states that the "Relief and Works Agency for Palestinian refugees" employs and provides benefits to terrorists and to criminals, it publishes unilateral political declarations and it funds textbooks that educate to discrimination. [35]

---

[34] http://www.jha.ac/articles/a135.htm

[35] Fixing UNRWA – The Washington Institute, James G. Lindsay, Policy Focus #91 | January   2009.

The folly and the waste of the UN are inconceivable. Instead of using its resources efficiently and dealing with human rights and regulating global issues, many of its departments are busy finding ways to condemn Israel time after time.

The differences between the UN Office of The High Commissioner for Refugees (UNHCR) and the UNRWA are not reflected only in manpower and in the budget, but also in the definition of "refugee". And gain, there is a definition for a "regular refugee" and there is a definition for a "Palestinian refugee".

MAKES NO SENSE!

Definition of a Palestinian refugee: Palestinian refugees are people whose habitual residence, from June 1946 until May 1948, was in Palestine, [36] and who have lost their homes and their livelihood as a result of the Arab-Israeli conflict in 1948. The definition of a "refugee" applies also to their descendents. [37]

The services of UNRWA are available to anyone who lives in the range of activity of the organization, who meets the definitions above and who is registered with the Agency as someone in need of assistance. The descendents of the original Palestinian refugees are also entitled to register as refugees. When the agency began to operate in 1950, it responded to the needs of about 750,000 Palestinian refugees. Today, 5 million Palestinian refugees are eligible for the services of UNRWA.

---

[36] In the previous chapter we have learned that the name of the place was Palestine by virtue of the British Mandate that chose to go back to this name that originates in the times of the destruction of the Second Temple.

[37] From Wikipedia, under the entry: "UNRWA"

While in the definition of a "regular refugee" it is mentioned that a refugee is a person who was forced to abandon his permanent residence, Palestinian refugees are people whose place of residence was Palestine from June 1946 until May 1948

There is a reason for everything. Why a Palestinian refugee is any person who lived in the territory under the British Mandate between 1946 and 1948?

Many immigrants flowed from Arab countries to Israel during those years. Immigrants who came to try their luck following the local economic growth that resulted directly from the Jewish immigration to Israel. Egyptian, Syrians and Lebanese families decided to try their luck and to immigrate to Palestine (a name given by the British during the British Mandate). These families settled in the area in 1945, but when the War of Independence broke out, they were forced to escape back to somewhere towards May-June 1948. Those too are considered Palestinian refugees. This is a march of folly, a falsification of history under an agenda that aims to put constant pressure for the destruction of the State of Israel, by promising a "just peace", and "the Right of Return", as the Palestinians demand.

MAKES NO SENSE!

One of the amusing falsifications in this situation is that there are refugees or their descendants who have integrated in the life of the country where they were born or to which they immigrated. They do not consider themselves as refugees, but in terms of UNRWA, they are still considered as Palestinian refugees in the full sense of the word.

As a result, a winning combination has been created of political interests and a radical agenda that does not enable to conclude a peace agreement with the Jewish State of Israel.

According to the conception of the Palestinians, any peace agreement will require a just solution to the eternal Palestinian problem, i.e., the settlements of about 5,000,000 refugees inside the State of Israel. An option that will destroy its Jewish character from within and will make the State of Israel a member in a confederacy of another 22 Arab countries.

MAKES NO SENSE!

The Palestinian refugee problem will not end until the State of Israel is destroyed! This is its purpose. Someone thinks I am exaggerating or bullshitting? Really?

During the War of Independence about 750 thousand Arabs have left, were expelled or evacuated. At the end of the war the State of Israel was left without ~~Judea and Samaria~~ the West Bank and the Gaza Strip. Not a single Jew was left in these areas! A simple calculation shows that over 65 years have passed since then, something like two and a half generations. It is likely that most of the original refugees have already died or that they are very old. In other words, how many are still alive out of the original 750 thousand? Today we are talking about their descendants, their grandchildren or even their great-grandchildren.

How it is possible that the great-grandchildren of refugees are still considered refugees?

At the end of World War II there were huge streams of refugees all over the world. Entire populations migrated across continents trying to find a new shelter for themselves. Some of them were forced to leave (like my parents who were expelled destitute from Iraq) and reached the desert wasteland of the State of Israel in 1951. If so, am I also a refugee? After all, my parents were refugees.

Do I have to exercise the right of return to Iraq with millions of other refugees, with the children of refugees and the grand-children of refugees? And I did not even know that I am a refugee. How many generations continue to be refugees? Is there not something in this situation that doesn't fit? When will it stop? Only when the State of Israel is wiped out?

At this rate, in 60 years the population of the great-grandchildren of the refugees will surpass the population of the USA today. And then what? They will continue to demand to exercise the right of return?

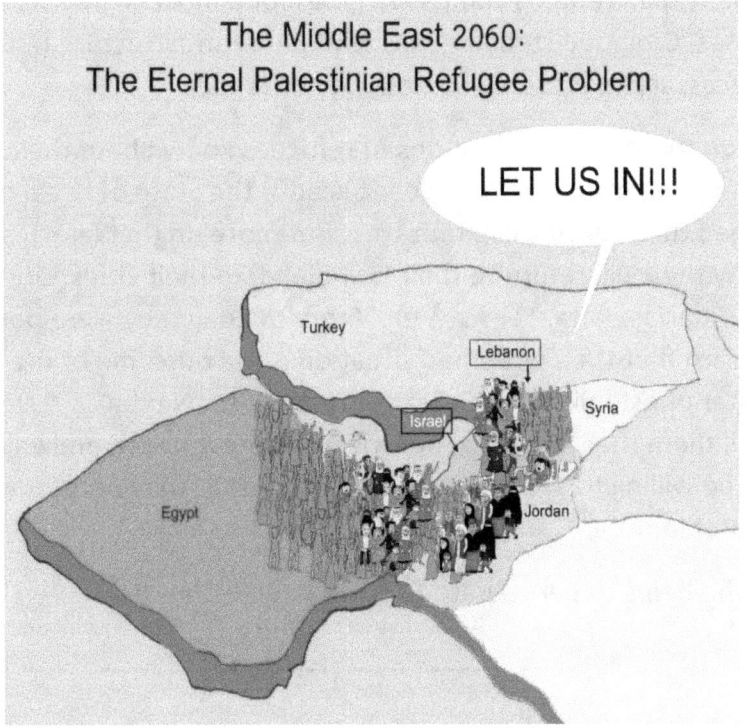

Rafik Al-Hariri, the Lebanese prime minister who was murdered, argued in an interview with channel MBC on February 5th, 1998:

"We do not want to fall into the trap of the resettlement of the Palestinians. This will lead to the assimilation of the refugees. The

Palestinians themselves have repeatedly rejected this approach, so that their distinction (as refugees) remains unchanged." [38]

A particularly big absurd is that in the areas of the Palestinian Authority there are still refugee camps. After all, this is supposed to be the Palestinian state, so why perpetuate the refugee camps?

What is a Palestinian refugee camp?

Unlike the refugees from Haiti or from Congo who sleep in tents or out in the open air and wait for daily relief of food and medications, the Palestinian refugee camps are cities for almost all intents and purposes. Crowded stone houses with poor infrastructure (after all it is necessary to preserve something authentic).

What do these new generations of refugees know about their fate? They know that they are refugees because the State of Israel has banished their forefathers (not true. But more on that later), and one day they will return to their homeland, to their cities: cities like Haifa, Tiberias, Jaffa, Tel-Aviv, etc. From the day they were born they learn that their wretched situation is the outcome of the "disaster of establishing the State of Israel the "Naqba". [39] No one will tell them that the Arab countries have never been and will never be willing to absorb them, and as a result they perpetuate their problem.

And who helps to perpetuate this "disaster"? The UN.

---

[38] http://www.peacefaq.com/palestinians.html

[39] From Wikipedia: Naqba ("the disaster") is the term used by the Arabs for the 1948 War of Independence when about 700,000 Arabs who lived in Israel fled, left or were expelled from their homes and settled in various Arab countries or in other places in Israel, in the West Bank and in the Gaza Strip, thus creating the Palestinian refugee problem, including the demand for the "Right of Return".

Think, for example, about immigrants that came to the United States. Has anyone heard of refugees who are living in the United States and who wish, after over 70 years since the end of World War II, to exercise the Right of Return to their countries in Europe, in Africa, in the Far East? After all, this is a ridiculous and far-fetched idea. Why, then, does it sound logical when it comes to the Palestinian refugees?

If we accept the definition of a refugee under the "UN Convention Relating to the Status of Refugees" [40] from 1951 one fact will stand out undisputedly: there is no Palestinian refugee problem. The Convention does not define a refugee as someone who received citizenship in the country of his domicile, and it also does not recognize the descendants of the refugee as refugees (since they receive citizenship in the country that absorbed them.)

The Arab countries refuse to grant citizenship to refugees, to their children and to their descendants. The exception is Jordan that allowed most of the refugees to get citizenship and to become regular citizens. The retired Legal Adviser of UNRWA James Lindsay said on this subject: "In Jordan, where 2 million Palestinian refugees reside, everybody, except for 167,000 persons, has Jordanian citizenship that enables him to enjoy government rights, such as education and health care". Lindsay maintained that subtracting these 2 million "refugees" will reduce their total number by 40%!!! [41]

---

[40] The Convention of all the refugees and not of the Palestinians; they have a separate Convention.

[41] http://en.wikipedia.org/wiki/Palestinian_refugee

Mathematically, the number of refugees cannot exceed the original number of about 750,000, but since the true purpose of UNRWA is to preserve at all costs the refugee problem, the number of the Palestinian refugees has grown astronomically, and they constitute the world's largest refugee population!

Even refugees who received citizenship in Arab countries, such as Jordan, that do not consider themselves as refugees, are still classified by the UNRWA as such, namely: refugees who do not know that they are refugees and do not want to be such.

MAKES NO SENSE!

It is important to understand, if Israel allows the "repatriation" of 5 million Palestinians, their balance in the population will increase to over 50% and will put an end to the Jewish state. This is what is called "A just peace and a just solution to the Palestinian refugee problem". [42] About that the Palestinians declare they are not going ever to give up.

---

[42] As has been said many times by Palestinian and by Arab leaders.

The main thing is that their hands are outstretched in peace! "I come in peace!"

A Solution for the Palestinian Refugee Problem

I come in peace.

Each year the Palestinian "Naqba" is commemorated, a disaster named the State of Israel that "created" the refugee problem. This day is "celebrated" at the UN on November 29th with ceremonies and speeches. [43]

But for some reason the Jewish "Naqba" is not commemorated. Does anyone know that about 1,000,000 Jews were banished from Arab countries when the Jewish State was established? Jews who have been living in these countries for hundreds and thousands of years, thriving communities, were forced to leave and leave behind their belongings. Did you hear about them? No. For example, my parents and their parents left behind wealth and property, which was nationalized by the Iraqi government. They arrived to the State of Israel penniless and had to start all over again. After 68 years of its existence, the results are impressive and I say that responsibly!

---

[43] This date is not accidental. On November 29th, 1947, the United Nations General Assembly voted to end the British Mandate and to establish in the Land of Israel two states – a Jewish state and an Arab state.

Why is this Naqba not commemorated? Why does the UN not dedicate a day of solidarity to the 1,000,000 Jewish refugees? Why is the Palestinian Naqba commemorated by the UN on the same day its members voted in 1947 in favor of establishing a Jewish state and an Arab state?

I surely do not want to plunder the priority rights of the Palestinian "Naqba", but still, let's talk a little about the Jewish "Naqba:

The Jewish Naqba:

While UNRWA estimates the number of Palestinian refugees who have left Israel in 1948 at about 750 thousand, it is estimated that about 1,000,000 Jews were banished destitute from the Arab countries in 1948. Their property was nationalized and they were forced to leave only with the clothes on.

I took the information regarding the creation of the Jewish refugee problem from an article quoted in Wikipedia: "Jewish exodus from Arab and Muslim lands".

A large part of the Jews in Arab countries were forced to leave their homeland against their will, due to personal insecurity and to the rise of Arab nationalism. Everybody had to sell or to abandon their property in favor of the state. Until 2002, the share of the Jewish refugees and their offspring in the population of the State of Israel was about 40%.

"The World Organization of Jews from Arab countries" (WOJAC) [44] estimated that the property left behind in the Arab countries exceeded $300 billion, or in numbers: $300,000,000,000. Jewish-owned lands were 4 times bigger than the total area of the State of Israel! Around 100,000 square kilometers.

---

[44] The organization was founded in 1975 and was accepted as a non-governmental organization to the UN. Its main goal was to ensure the legitimate rights of the Jews to indemnifications for the assets they left behind and that was nationalized by the Arab countries. The organization stopped its activities in 1999.

The Organization believes that the decision to banish the Jews from the Arab countries was a deliberate decision made by the Arab League. The Arab world consists of 22 countries.

In these countries there were ancient Jewish communities from the time of the Babylonian exile, dated to the 6th century, i.e., about 1,000 years before the first Arab was born!!!

Do you understand? Whole communities have been uprooted from their homelands and forced to wander in destitute surrounded by waves of hatred, by political persecutions and by Arab nationalism. These communities were founded and have been in existence in those areas 1,000 years before Mohammed was born and founded Islam!

In April 1941, a military coup took place in Iraq. The British had to regain control by force, and at the end of May the mission succeeded. The incited Iraqi mob found an outlet for their rage in organizing a pogrom [45] against the Jews during which 179 men, women and children were massacred.

From a personal angle, I present here a firsthand testimony of the massacre, that of my mother:

...When I spoke about it with my mother, she could hardly hide the feelings of horror that have been haunting her since childhood. She was just over 3 years old, about the same age as my two-years-old second daughter. The innocence, the love of life, the curiosity and the joy were cut off all at once. One night, the family of my mother heard sudden violent hammer blows on the door accompanied by shouts: "Slaughter the Jews". My mother and her family were petrified. The fact that their house was in proximity to the local mosque, saved them.

---

[45] Acts of destruction, of massacres and of murder.

The Imam of the mosque, who heard the violent hammer blows on the door and the shouts: "Slaughter the Jews", ran to the house, stood at the doorway and blocked the mob with his body. The door was already broken.

During the night, the Imam members guarded the house and the lives of my mother and her family. The pogrom continued throughout the next day, and ended only towards the evening, when the British intervened (Iraq was part of the British Empire).

Her aunt, though, was unfortunate. They broke into her home, looted everything, killed her and threw her down the stairs like a carcass. Is that a memory a 3-year-old girl should bear throughout her life?

Pogroms in which Jews lost their lives happened, among others, in Libya and Egypt in 1945, in Yemen, Bahrain and Syria in 1947, in Iraq and Morocco in 1948. At the same time, the Arab countries began "encouraging" Jewish immigration to Israel. The phenomenon of pogroms against Jewish communities spread in the Arab world. In Libya, their citizenship was revoked, in Iraq their property was nationalized and Jews were banished expelled without being allowed to take their property.

Of all the 1,000,000 Jewish refugees, 680,000 came to the State of Israel. The rest immigrated to Europe and to the United States. The hundreds of thousands of refugees who streamed into the State of Israel were housed in "tent cities" and later in absorption camps called "Ma`abarot". The last "Ma`abara" was closed in 1963. The refugee population gradually integrated into Israeli society. This is a huge accomplishment by any standard, since it was achieved without assistance from the UN or its agencies.

A Jewish refugee absorption camp in Beit Lid. [46]

Photographer: Zoltan Kluger, 1949.

How did the State of Israel manage to deal with the problem of the Jewish refugees who constituted a significant part of its population, without resorting to the UN Relief Agencies? On the other hand, how is it that the Palestinian refugees need of a Relief Agency that is dedicated exclusively to them, an Agency that for over 65 years has failed to deal with the Palestinian refugee problem?

---

[46] This Ma`abara was one of the 7 refugee camps that were built in Israel until a solution for the refugee housing problem was found. This Ma`abara was the largest in the State of Israel.

How did the State of Israel with its meager resources succeed, during the 60s of the last century, to solve the problem of about 680,000 refugees while UNRWA, with all its resources, has failed?

MAKES NO SENSE!

This is probably the perfect proof that the purpose of UNRWA is to preserve the refugee problem and not to solve it at all.

In fact, there are 3 fundamental differences between the 2 "Naqbas":

1. In 1948, with the Declaration of Independence of the State of Israel, the Arab countries started a war of destruction against the State, while the local Arab population collaborated with them. Some Arabs left voluntarily with the encouragement of their leaders, some were forced to escape. By contrast, the Jewish communities in the Arab countries were loyal to their countries where they have lived for thousands of years, and were expelled with the rise of Arab nationalism just because they were Jewish.
2. The Jewish refugee problem was solved by the tiny State of Israel that absorbed   680,000 Jews without the help of the UN and its institutions. The Palestinian refugee problem is perpetuated by the UN and its institutions.
3. The Palestinian refugee problem is rooted in the Palestinian people and in the Arab world and it serves as a central narrative in their lives, while the Jewish refugee problem has never been utilized politically by the Jews or by the State of Israel.

The State of Israel assumed responsibility for the Jewish refugee problem that it did not create. The Jews were not hostile. They were loyal to their countries, they assisted to develop their countries and they contributed to them much more than their proportionate share in the population. As a "prize" for that, they were banished and their property was nationalized.

Why do the Arabs and the Arab countries refuse to assume responsibility for the refugee problem that they have created? Responsibility for a hostile population that has declared war, for a population that was urged by the Arab leadership and by its encouragement to leave?

Is that the problem of the State of Israel? Not at all!

Irwin Cotler, a lawyer who specializes in Human Rights and the former Minister of Justice of Canada (2003-2006), referred to the migration of the refugees as a "double Naqba". He criticized the Arab countries for their refusal to recognize the Jewish state. Beyond their attempt to destroy the Jewish state, the Arab countries "punished" their Jewish residents by deporting them destitute. The outcome was a "double Naqba", not only the Palestinian Arabs suffered by the creation of a refugee problem but the Jewish population that has been banished from the Arab countries as well. Thus another refugee problem was created, a much less known – the problem of the Jewish refugees from Arab countries.

The following table shows details of the extermination of entire Jewish communities that existed for thousands of years before the advent of Islam and pan-Arabism: [47]

---

[47] Pam-Arabism is a movement that advocates the political, the social and the economic unification of the Arab people and the Arab countries in the Middle East. The term is closely connected to Arab nationalism. Traditionally, pan-Arabism has adopted a secular, social and anti-Western identity. From Wikipedia under the entry: "pan-Arabism".

The Jewish population in Arab countries in 1948 compared to 2008:

Country or region	The Jewish population in 1948	The Jewish population in 2008
Aden	8,000	0
Algeria	140,000	0
Bahrain	550-600	Less than 50
Egypt	75,000-80,000	Less than 100
Lebanon	5,000-20,000	About 40
Libya	35,000-38,000	0
Iraq	135,000-140,000	Less than 100
Morocco	250,000-265,000	2,500-4,000
Sudan	350	0
Syria	15,000-30,000	Less than 300
Tunisia	50,000-105,000	About 1,500
Yemen	45,000-55,000	Less than 350
Afghanistan	5,000	1
Kurdistan	50,000	Small number
Iran	70,000-150,000	25,000-40,000
Pakistan	2,000-2,500	About 200
Turkey	80,000	18,000-23,000
Total	**966,000-1,170,000**	**48,000-69,000**

According to the definition of the UN Relief and Works Agency for Palestine Refugees, I am considered a refugee and I am entitled to an appropriate compensation from Iraq. My parents were refugees who were forced to leave Iraq. They arrived here destitute and had to start all over again. Do I feel like a refugee? No. I was born here and this is my country. My parents worked hard to enable themselves and me a reasonable standard of living. When I was little I felt a shortage, but I did not hear my parents complain about it or blame anyone, although they did feel frustrated. My parent looked ahead to being productive and not to perpetuating the problem.

By the standards of UNRWA, the number of Jewish refugees in the world today is estimated between 4-5 million refugees. But you will not hear a word about it, because the problem was solved, because nobody tried to perpetuate it or to derive political gain from it.

And what about the rest of the refugees in the world? Why are they in the shadow?

There is no doubt, the world is hypocrite, the leaders are hypocrites the UN is hypocrite!

And you know the truth already!

I asked my mother to prepare a list of the property and of the land owned by her family and by my late father's family. Regarding my father's family, my mother had only partial information. Following, in brief, is a list of the property that the families of my mother and of my father were forced to leave behind:

Property owned my mother's family:

Basra region, southern Iraq:

- 4 Private houses.
- 3 Gigantic palm plantations.

Bagdad region, central Iraq:

- Her parents` 3 private houses.
- A big 4-story house that was the family residence.
- A 4 acres lot in "New Bagdad".
- 4 stores registered in the name of her mother.
- A private house in the Chanuni neighborhood.
- The Scheherazade cinema near the Saadon Park owned 50 % by her mother and 50% by other partners.

Partial information about the property left by my late father's family:

- A house they used to rent in the area called Alawi
- The house they lived in.

Today there are no Palestinian refugees, there are the descendants of the refugees: like myself, like all the children of refugees or of immigrants who are born in their country. They are no longer refugees. Remember that.

Let`s check together who created the problem which, from the point of view of the Arabs and of the Palestinians, "must" be resolved by Israel in order to achieve a "just" solution to the eternal refugee problem.

Ralph Garawai, former Director General of UNRWA, said in August 1958: "The Arab countries are not interested to resolve the refugee problem. They are interested to leave it as a bleeding wound, as a front against the United Nations and as a weapon against the State of Israel. Arab leaders do not give a damn about the refugees and it does not interest them whether they live or die". [48]

"The Economist" [49] reported on October 2nd, 1948: "Out of 62,000 Arabs of Haifa, between 5,000 to 6,000 remained. They had many reasons to leave.

---

[48] http://www.middleeastpiece.com/arabrefugees_whystillhere.html

[49] News Magazine (newspaper) based in London. It is considered one of the most important and influential newspaper in the world.

But in fact an important factor in their decision to leave was the calls broadcasted on the airwaves by Arab leaders that urged them to leave....It was clear, in fact, that the Arabs who chose to stay in Haifa and who benefited from Jewish custody were traitors". [50]

The "Arab Middle East" radio station located in Cyprus, broadcasted on April 3rd. 1949: "We must not forget that the Arab Higher National Committee encouraged the refugees to leave their homes in Jaffa, Haifa and Jerusalem". [51]

Edward Selim Atiyah, former Secretary of the Arab League in London, referred in his book "The Arabs: The Origins, Present Conditions, and Prospects of the Arab World", 1955, to the origin of the Palestinian refugee problem, p. 183: "This mass emigration was due, partly, to the belief of the Arabs, encouraged by the boastings of an unrealistic Arabic press and the irresponsible utterances of some of the Arab leaders, that the defeat of the Jews by the armies of the Arab countries is a matter of a few weeks only. Then the Palestinians will be able to return and claim possession of the whole country". [52]

---

[50] The Palestinian Refugees, http://www.jewishvirtuallibrary.org/jsources/History/refugee/html by Mitchell Bard.

[51] http://www.jewishfederations.org/page.aspx?id=121275

[52] http://www.jewishfederations.org/page.aspx?id=121275

The TIME magazine published on May 3rd 1948, that the mass evacuation was inflamed by fear and was partly because it came as an order by Arab leaders who left Haifa behind as a ghost town. The leaders hoped that the desertion of the Arab workers will paralyze Haifa. [53]

The American Journalist Kenneth W. Bilby referred in his book "New Star in the Near East", 1950, on pages 30-31, to the problem of the Palestinian refugees: "The mass exodus was inflamed by many Arab leaders, such as Hajj Amin al-Husseini, the exiled Mufti of Jerusalem who was a distinct pro-Nazi, and by the Arab Higher National Committee. They reckoned that the flux of refugees to the Arab countries will inspire them to make a bigger effort to invade and attack the Jews, and when they are thrown into the sea, the Palestinian Arabs will be able to return and benefit from a compensation in the form of the Jewish property". [54]

Emil Gohari, Secretary of the Arab Higher National Committee, the official leadership of the Palestinian Arabs, said in the Daily Telegraph (the Beirut newspaper) on September 6th 1948: "I do not wish to disagree with anyone, only to help the refugees. The fact is that the refugee problem was created as a direct result of the acts of hostility taken by the Arab countries following the Partition Plan and the establishment of a Jewish state. The Arab countries agreed unanimously on this policy, and therefore they must cooperate in resolving the problem". [55]

---

[53] http://www.jewishfederations.org/page.aspx?id=121275

[54] A History of the Israel-Palestinian conflict, Mark Tessler, p. 306.

[55] Israel and its Future: Analysis and Suggestions, Michael Anbar, p.56.

The following was published in the Jordanian newspaper "Palestine" on February 19th 1949: "The Arab countries encouraged the Arab Palestinians to leave their homes in order to make way for the invasion by the armies of the Arab countries". [56]

The Iraqi Prime Minister at the time, Nuri al-Said, spoke about the matter and said: "We will crush the country with our guns and will erase each place where Jews are looking for shelter. The Arabs must take their women and children to safer places until the fighting ceases". [57]

Mahmoud Abbas (Abu Mazen), Chairman of the Palestinian Authority, said in March 1976 in the official newspaper of the PLO, in Beirut: "Arab armies entered Palestine in order to protect the Palestinians from the Zionist tyranny, but instead they abandoned them, they forced them to immigrate and to leave their homeland, and threw them into prisons similar to the ghettos in which the Jews lived". [58]

Pay attention that the references and the quotes are about the Arabs of Palestine and not about the Palestinians, because at that time the whole region that was under the rule of the Mandate was the region of Palestine and all the inhabitants of the region were called Palestinians. There were Jewish Palestinians and there were Arab Palestinians. Only after the establishment of the State of Israel the name Palestinians was appropriated exclusively to the Arabs of the Region.

---

[56] Fast Facts on the Middle East Conflict, Randall Price, p. 78.
[57] http://www.science.co.il/Arab-Israeli-conflict/Refugee.asp
[58] http://israelipalestinian.procon.org/view.answers.php?questionsID=481

Mahmoud Abbas (Abu Mazen), the "moderate" partner, lays the responsibility for the Palestinian refugee problem on the Arab armies. Therefore, it is the responsibility of the Arab countries and it is only just that the Arab countries will bear the burden of addressing the problem. Nonetheless, he repeatedly reminds in his many speeches the need for a "just solution of the Palestinian refugee problem" by claiming the "Right of Return" as a basic condition for any agreement.

The Arabs cultivate the separate Palestinian nationalism and the myth of "restoring the rights of the Palestinian people" – on Israel`s territory and in its place. The Palestinian National claim is the most distinct expression of the unwillingness of the Arab countries to recognize the legitimate existence of the State of the Jewish people.

While the State of Israel fully absorbed within its boundaries the Jews from the Arab countries, from North Africa and from the Persian Gulf: in housing, in employment, in education, in culture and in economy, the Arab countries and the Arab League perpetuated the Arab refugee problem as a political weapon in their war against the State of Israel.

The world continues to support financially the maintenance of the refugees in the Arab countries, in ~~Judea and Samaria~~ the West Bank and in the Gaza Strip. With the billions of dollars that have been poured over the years, it would have been possible already to rehabilitate the last of the refugees and more.

The Palestinians` yearning for peace

Here are, in brief, the results of the incessant propaganda, product of the Palestinians, the Arab countries and the new anti-Semitism (just remember that propaganda creates de-legitimization in the long run):

According to the propaganda, the Palestinians yearn for peace, their hand is outstretched in peace time after time, but the "despicable and cowardly" people living in Zion reject it. The yearning of the Palestinian for peace is so strong, that they are willing to die as martyrs for it. Their yearning for peace is so strong, that no endless songs have ever been written about it, people are not named after it, streets and public institutions are not named after it. But for peace you need a partner.

On the opposite side are the "despicable and evil conspirators" Zionists. The Zionists turn them down. There is no doubt that the Jews living in Zion are not interested in a just and sustainable peace, and it seems that all they are trying to do is sabotage the efforts for peace.

For that reason Israel is one of the most hated countries in the world.

The following graph illustrates well what the international public opinion thinks regarding the negative contribution of Israel to the world:

The perception of the countries around the world

60	21	19	Germany
57	21	22	Britain
50	28	22	France
46	28	26	Brazil
48	24	28	The European Union
50	20	30	Japan
39	24	37	India
42	19	39	United States
42	16	42	China
30	24	46	Russia
24	28	48	Israel
18	23	59	Pakistan
19	22	59	North Korea
18	22	60	Iran

Negative UnKnown Psitive

100%   80%   60%   40%   20%   0%

According to a public opinion poll of the Economist in 2014 [59]

According to the propaganda, Israel not only "does not" want peace, but it has settled on vast occupied territories.

---

[59]   http://www.economist.com/news/briefing/21610312-pummelling-gaza-has-cost-israel-sympathy-not-just-europe-also-among-americans

The territories are so vast, that they push the Arab nation to the margins of the Middle East.

The Jews have occupied vast territories and they keep the population in these areas under conditions such as they themselves have not experienced in the Holocaust (which never happened).

The Jews are committing "crimes against humanity" in those territories, while trampling human   dignity and human quality. "Death marches" are carried out throughout the Gaza Strip. "Hit Squads" of Israeli soldiers are putting to death tens of thousands of Palestinians. "Death camps" are built throughout the Strip, while Palestinians are led across Israel in freight trains. After traveling for days and nights they are sorted according to their potential to be of use to the superior Jewish race. The Jews have no aspirations for peace at all. No wonder that Israel occupies a significant part of the global news.

Stop the Holocaust in Gaza! What is this if not a contempt! A girl holds a banner with a doll, saying   "Stop Gaza Holocaust", on January 11, 2009, in Brussels, after a demonstration by 30,000 people against the ongoing assault by Israel on Gaza.
AFP PHOTO / BELGA PHOTO / BENOIT DOPPAGNE

Let's see how the Palestinians educate the next generation for a better future, "for peace". [(60)]

A lesson in the laws of peace for the sake of the younger Palestinian generation. A devoted mother shows her son how to get ready for the coming peace.

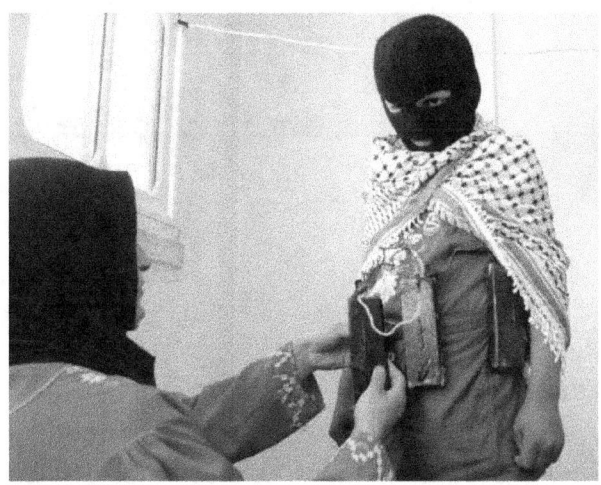

[(60)] This picture was shown on the Facebook page of Fatah alongside an imaginary dialogue between a child who is sent to die, and the mother who encourages it. "Why me and not you?" the child asks his mother innocently, and she answers him that she will continue to have children "for Palestine". Translation by the research institution "Palestinian Media Watch".
http://www.palwatch.org.il

His parents already know his destiny when he grows up...... [61]

AP Photo/Israeli Army/HO

Education for "peace" begins in infancy. Generations of Palestinians are educated in the values of hatred, death and vengeance while ignoring the facts and rewriting history. As part of the curriculum, the Palestinian children learn today about denying the Holocaust, about their historical homeland that was stolen by Western imperialism and on the hope to return to the stolen homeland, namely the whole state of Israel.

The Palestinians have been taught that an Israeli State does not exist. The brain washing begins in infancy and shapes the future generation of Palestinians as a militant generation that grows up with the sense of deprivation due to the robbery of their land by the "Zionist occupiers", following a Holocaust that never occurred.

---

[61]   The picture of the baby dressed as a suicide bomber is a photo of a Palestinian baby wearing an explosive   belt-like device found during a search by IDF soldiers in Hebron on June 29th 2002. See further details about this in Wikipedia under the entry: "The picture of the baby dressed as a suicide bomber".

The propaganda book "The Protocols of the Elders of Zion" [62] has become for them a solid fact.

These children or teenagers do not have the obvious access to the various media or to other languages, in the same way as people who reside in democratic countries have. The television is tuned to Arab channels or to the Hamas channel and the programs for children and for teenagers that are supposed to show contents suitable for children, show contents about the conflict and the way to solve it (Jihad and martyrdom). Hundreds of Web sites in Arabic are spread in the internet, which contain virulent and anti-Semitic content. The press and the children books talk about the hope to return to the lost homeland that has been stolen. The children, brainwashed by tens of thousands of hours of hatred, do not know anything else. A different alternative, exposed to children in the Western world, does not exist for them and they are unaware of it.

MAKES NO SENSE!

I know it sounds bizarre, but those Palestinian teenagers and children do not know anything except that their country has been stolen, and they have to get it back forcefully from the infidels who took it over.

---

[62] The Protocols of the Elders of Zion is the most wide-spread anti-Semitic document in the world, which had a huge impact on the history of the 20th century and on the fate of the Jews. This fraudulent fabricated text was one of the main books of the Nazis and was used as a justification for their deeds. To this day, anti-Semitic elements make great use of it in their fight against the Jews and the State of Israel. Copies of the book are disseminated through governmental organizations of some Arab countries, even for free, and through the internet. From Wikipedia.

Let me prove it to you:

The pictures were taken from The Intelligence and Terrorism Information Center in the internet and from the Palestinian media watch.

Children are sent to watch dead babies in order to instill in them hatred for Israel (the picture was published in the Al-Fatah website, the June edition 2009). (63)

By the way, not always there is a connection between the death and the State of Israel and its army. It happens more than once that dead people and casualties from other places and other events are displayed and attributed to Israel.

---

(63) More details about it are available on the website of The Intelligence and Terrorism Information Center at: http://www.terrorism-info.org.il/he/article/18206 under the article: "The Hatred Industry: Hamas continues to instill messages of hatred and violence against Israel among the children of the Gaza Strip", 07/10/2009.

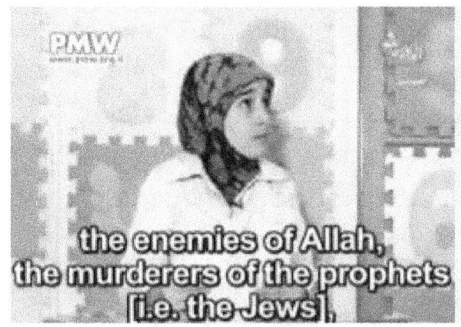

Nahool the bee invokes to follow the course of suicide bombing as revenge against the enemies of Islam and the murderers of the prophets (the Jews), the killers of the innocent children.
Al-Aqsa channel, July 13th, 2007 (courtesy of the Palestinian Media Watch, www.palwatch.org).

Another picture from a lovely children`s program suitable for the young age:

Nassur the bear: "We want to slaughter them (the Jews), so that they will be wiped out of our land, right?" (The photo is taken from the Hamas Al-Aqsa channel on September 22nd, courtesy of Palestinian Media Watch, www.palwatch.org.).

An internet newspaper for children is published in the city of Londonistan in Britain: The Al-Fatah website, an online newspaper of the Hamas (which can be reached through the Hamas website

Palestine-info), is published every week in London. This newspaper is intended for children and serves the Hamas as another means to instill the values of hatred of Israel and of the Jewish people, to encourage the use of terror and of violence, and to implement the radical- Islamic ideology of Hamas among the young generation: Following are a few examples:

Al-Fatah, the January 2009 edition: a picture titled "Gaza – Allah will bring your victory". The picture shows a child dressed in the military uniform of the Izz ad-Din al-Qassam brigades, the military wing of the Hamas terror organization. The boy carries the Palestinian flag. In the article, it says: "Palestine is the problem of all the Muslims, even if they are at the end of the world. Tell them about the land of Palestine that is an Islamic land and will stay like that forever. Therefore, no matter what the Zionists will do, they will destroy and shed blood, they have no right to exist there. Tell them about their forefathers and about your forefathers and separate between them. They have violated agreements, they have killed innocent people, they have turned lie into truth and truth into lie. As for our forefathers, they are mighty and great, they fulfill agreements. Tell them about the slyness of the Jews towards the prophet Muhammad, a slyness that will continue until the end of time. There can be no trust in the Jews, no matter how much they try to prove their innocence". [64]

---

[64] http://www.terrorism-info.org.il/he/articleprint.aspx?id=18206

Please note that this is about Jews, not about Israelis. As far as they are concerned this is a religious war. There will be no redemption until the last Jew is wiped out. Thus, even if the State of Israel decides to cancel itself and send all its residents to Mars, the Jews will still be persecuted and obliterated, to the last one.

These slanderous writings are published all the time in enlightened democratic countries. Under the cover of a different, unknown language, the haters of the West, the haters of Israelis/Jews are able to disseminate unhindered their doctrine to a new Muslim generation that was brought up on hatred and on religious radicalism. Europe's hypocrisy regarding its attitude to Jews creates a boomerang effect, because the ideology does not consider only Israel or the Jews as the enemies of Islam, but all the infidels wherever they are.

It won't be long, and regardless of the Jews/Israelis, and the hatred will be directed also against the hosting countries whose leaders will try to understand where they went wrong (their integration in the country, deprivation, discrimination etc....). It will take them a long time to understand that they were wrong by hosting an ideology that seeks to replace them demographically and by force.

Kindergarten graduation ceremonies are always an occasion for partying. The happy parents prepare for it in advance, toward the time when their little ones complete another year in kindergarten. The children are looking forward to the vacation and they are excited knowing that they have grown in a year. The excited parents are sitting on chairs waiting for the moment to see their little ones sing or dance and their hearts will expand with pride. This is a universal picture shared by all mankind.

Among the Palestinians as well there is excitement, but the content of the expected show is slightly different.

On June 3rd, 2009 a website affiliated with the Islamic Jihad (Pal Today), published photos from the graduation ceremony of children who finished their studies at the Dar Alhoda Society. The ceremony was held at the Rashad Al-Shawar Center in Gaza. In this ceremony, one of many, the kindergarten children are dressed in uniforms and carry toy guns. During the ceremony they clash with IDF soldiers and kill them.

Following is a selection of photos from the ceremony: [65]

Shooting towards IDF soldiers

A "victory dance" by kindergarten children around bodies of IDF soldiers lying on the floor in the center of the picture (with small-scale Israeli flags on their clothing). The kindergarten children are carrying Palestinian flags and a replica of the Dome of the Rock (a symbol of the liberation of Jerusalem).

Proud family members are present at the performance by kindergarten children. On the left: a child wearing a ribbon of the Jerusalem Brigades, the military-terrorist wing of the Islamic Jihad in Palestine.

If these are the contents and the show that children perform toward their graduation from kindergarten, what does that say about the parents?

The mind of children is innocent and pure and it is very easy to influence it. A systematic education of this kind is one of the most serious crimes against humanity. These children, who could get an education for a better future, are programmed to hate and to wish for martyrdom.

---

(65) From articles appearing on the website: http://www.terrorism-info.org.il

What is the sin of these children that their parents and their leaders have given them up, have renounced their childhood and to dedicate all of them to continue "the struggle against the Zionist occupier"? Is it possible to make peace with them? I doubt it.

These are only very few examples from the hate industry that is brainwashing the minds of millions of Muslim children around the world. These children grow up on one undisputable truth. The moral and the ideological foundations and the justifications for Jihad are served well chewed into the mouths of these children, who are thirsty for information about the world they were born into. The belief in change does not stem from the desire to develop and to improve, but from the uncontrollable desire to kill the Jews.

These pictures were taken straight from the future. A gloomy future in which the soul of children is corrupted. Children who will grow up to be cruel, full of hate and brainwashed. Would it be possible to do something? I doubt it.

Remember: the moment the Arab countries and the extremist organizations decide to lay down their arms – there will be peace.

Now it is time to check the Israelis. According to the propaganda, Israel has no respect for agreements, Israel is aggressive and Israel does not want peace but conquest.

Judge for yourselves:

Streets named peace (Shalom): in almost every major city in Israel there is a street named "peace - Shalom".

- "The Shalom Road" in Tel-Aviv is a major horizontal traffic route that crosses the city of Tel-Aviv.
- "The Shalom Road" is a traffic route in the city of Be'er Sheva as well.

- There is "The Shalom street" in Haifa, in Mevasseret Zion and in Tiberias.

In the Palestinian Authority streets and squares are named after suicide bombers.

Songs of peace: many songs of peace have been composed and instilled in the heart of the Israeli citizen and he sings them in almost every significant ceremony. I will present some of them in order to illustrate the yearning of the Jewish people for peace.

I was born for peace – Uzi Hitman

I was born to the melodies
And to the songs of all the countries
I was born to the language and also to the place
To the few to the many that will lend a hand for peace.

I was born for the peace just let it arrive
I was born for the peace just let it come
I was born for the peace just let it appear
I want I want to be already at it.

I was born to the dream
In it I see that peace will come
I was born to the wish and the belief
That here it comes after thirty years.

I was born for the peace just let it arrive
I was born for the peace just let it come
I was born for the peace just let it appear
I want I want to be already at it.

I was born to a nation of two thousand years
To a reserved land with a patch of sky

And she watches and sees here rises the day
It is a beautiful time, this is peace time.

I was born for the peace just let it arrive
I was born for the peace just let it come
I was born for the peace just let it appear
I want I want to be already at it.

We brought you peace
A folk song
Lyrics and melody: folk

We brought you peace
We brought you peace
We brought you peace
We brought peace, peace
Be peace upon you.

A song for peace
Miri Aloni
Lyrics: Yankele Rotblit
Melody: Yair Rosenblum

Let the sun rise
Let the morning shine,
The purest of prayers
Will not bring us back.

He whose candle was put out
And he was buried in the earth,
No bitter cry will wake him up
And bring him back here.

No one will bring us back

From a dark bottom pit,
Here no joy of triumph
Nor songs of praise
Will be of any help.

Therefore, just sing a song for peace
Don`t whisper a prayer
Better sing a song for peace
With a loud shout.

Let the sun penetrate
Through the flowers.
Do not look back,
Allow to rest those who are gone.

Lift your eyes with hope,
Not through arms sights
Sing a song of love
And not of wars.

Do not say a day will come –
Bring forth the day!
Because it is not a dream
And in all the squares
Hail to the peace!

Therefore, Just sing a song for peace…………..

Peace on Israel
The Effi Netzer group
Lyrics: Dudu Barak
Melody: Effi Netzer

Lit a light in the streets and sing a song in the town
Tomorrow over all the hopes a bright day will dawn
Then from their dovecotes thousands of white doves will fly high

And a sun clearer than gold will call out of a cloud.

Peace, peace, peace on Israel
Say, say songs of praise, peace, peace on Israel.

When a golden day shines on the mount and on the hill
Stop the fire and the fight, warriors
Adorn yourselves with thousands of shades garlands and come
singing
With all the town girls to the lit city.

Peace, peace, peace on Israel.....

If by tomorrow peace will come until the end of time
From the plateau to Mount Nevo light up the bonfires
Then mount to mount will greet with peace and a big light will shine
And a new day will rise tomorrow all over the people of Israel.

Peace, peace, peace on Israel.....

Maker of Peace
The Gevatron
Lyrics: words of a prayer
Melody: Nurit Hirsh

Maker of Peace in heaven above
Will make peace for us
And for all the people of Israel
And say, say Amen.

He will make peace, will make peace
Peace for us and for all Israel
He will make peace, will make peace
Peace for us and for all Israel.

The curriculum in the educational institutions in Israel: includes learning the Arabic language, social studies, democracy, civics studies, and political science. The curriculum encourages dialogues among the students and between the students and their teachers. The introduction of opinions and criticism are the cornerstones of democracy. The right for self-criticism, for inner judgment is not suppressed.

Painful concessions: The people of Israel strive for peace; the State of Israel has made many concessions in exchange for promises that have been violated time after time. The State of Israel has conceded areas that are 3 times larger than its territory hers in order to achieve peace.

In 1967, when a defensive war was imposed on the State of Israel, Israel conquered vast areas in Sinai, in the Golan Heights and ~~Judea and Samaria~~ and the West Bank. The State of Israel conceded half of the Sinai Peninsula in order to get a cold peace with Egypt. Israel was willing even to withdraw from the whole of the Golan Heights, which is a strategic asset since it is a mountain range overlooking the entire northern part of Israel.

If anyone thinks that this is a common thing to do, check the history of the United States, of Europe and of the Middle East. The United States conquered vast areas of Mexico in the war that took place in 1846-1848. [66] California, Nevada, Utah, Arizona, parts of Wyoming, Colorado and New Mexico became an integral part of the United States.

MAKES NO SENSE!

---

[66] http://en.wikipedia.org/wiki/Mexican-American_War

Even Syria, that declared that there will be no peace with Israel until it receives the entire Golan Heights to the last inch, conceded to Turkey an area 4 times larger than the Golan Heights in the Alexandretta region. [67]

In my opinion, the biggest bungling is the fundamental misunderstanding that the Arab/Palestinian leadership has no intent to make peace.

This is a leadership that has been educating many generations to hate and to deny the existence of an entire country, a country that does not even exist for this leadership on the maps, and instead of creating for the next generation hope for a better future, the future generation is educated to believe that its future depends on the destruction of the Jewish state that stole and looted its land and its rights.

Rewriting history, combined with extreme religious elements and a justification to fight against the "colonial entity", produces a brained- washed generation with infinitesimal control over historical facts.

On November 5th, 2010, a senior Hamas official delivered a hateful anti-Semitic speech against the Jews [68] — note, not against the Israelis, but against Jews wherever they are.

In his speech, he describes how throughout history, the French, the British and the Germans deported and killed Jews because of their exploitative, intrigant and loathsome character and the conclusion finally was inevitable:
"There is no place for you among us, and you have no future among the nations of the world. You are headed to annihilation."

---

[67] http://en.wikipedia.org/wiki/Hatay_Province
[68] http://globalmbreport.org/?p=3605

He meant and believed every word.

They make sure to spread this message constantly and to use it for brainwashing as many brains as possible. This is a religious war that an Islam believer must execute according to the will of God.

The Hamas platform is saturated with the same hatred, yet it is the Israelis who "appose peace", the Israelis who "slaughter the people in Gaza". Ask judge Goldstone [69], he will be happy to tell you about it.

These minds, that are subjected to a malicious, massive and continues propaganda, cannot examine it themselves because they are living in a totalitarian regime which prevails in the Gaza Strip. The Palestinians are interested in a peace process and not in a peace agreement. The peace process has always led to concession and to gestures of good will on the part of Israel, but each gesture was perceived as a weakness.

On March 22nd, 2010 when there was an escalation in the activities of the Palestinian against Israel, the IDF responded. When I was at work, the Sky News channel was broadcasting all day. Every fifteen minutes approximately the words Israel, soldiers, rocks, were mentioned and on the screen Palestinians were seen throwing rocks on the soldiers. During the whole day pictures from ~~Judea and Samaria~~ the West Bank were broadcasted. On that day also a few missiles were fired toward Israeli cities from the Gaza Strip, but that was not covered at all. From the pictures that were broadcasted, it was clear who the weak was and who was the strong.

---

[69] From Wikipedia: on April 3rd, 2009 Richard J. Goldstone was appointed Head of the UN Fact Finding Mission on the Gaza Conflict, established to investigate the activities of the IDF during the Gaza war and the actions of the Hamas that led to the operation.

On that day the UN Secretary General as well visited our region and expressed his concern about the situation in the Gaza Strip. On the other hand, he did not refer at all to the issue of Gilad Shalit, the kidnapped soldier who was held in the Strip contrary to all the international conventions. He referred in one sentence to the shooting that has been going on for years on Israeli cities, but he expressed concern about the security barrier, that was meant to prevent the infiltration of suicide bombers into the center of Israel. The Secretary General is South Korean, and one of the most fortified security fences in the world is the one between North Korea and South Korea. The Secretary General had nothing to say about this.

MAKES NO SENSES!

It can be argued that Israel is successful. It is strong and its residents enjoy a Western standard of living. On the other hand, the Palestinians are wretched they live in despair, with no hope or future of a better life.

True. Israel has managed to thrive, thanks to and in spite of the circumstances and the enemies that have aspired to destroy it since the date of its its establishment. But, is this not proof of the joy of life and the sanctification of life? And what about the Palestinians? Yasser Arafat [70] was a terrorist who led the region into a mighty bloodbath. For his deeds he won the Nobel Prize for Peace. During his life he managed to accumulate huge amounts of money most of which were donations contributed by many organizations in the world in aid to Palestinian. Part of the donations were indeed passed on to their destination, but most of them remained with the well connected.

---

[70] Head of the Palestinian Authority since its inception until his death.

Even today, Hamas receives donations from Europe, the continent which the Hamas considers as the next stronghold of Islam. A lot of money is pumped into the Gaza Strip to build an army, many funds are allocated to purchase weapons. Ships loaded with weapons leave Iranian harbors toward the Gaza Strip. Just imagine what would have happened if the funds invested in building a layout for the destruction of Israel, were channeled to growth, to education and to rehabilitation. What a beautiful gem the Gaza Strip would have turned into.

Israel has never asked for the Gaza Strip, but it was obliged to accept it from the Egyptians with   the signing of the Peace Agreement with Egypt in 1979. Following the unilateral withdrawal from the Gaza Strip in 2005, the State of Israel evacuated all its soldiers and citizens and retreated to the borders of 1967. Israel left behind agricultural greenhouses in the Gush Katif that could constitute leverage for economic development in the Gaza Strip. Today, the greenhouses are ruined and abandoned. Hatred is blinding and it harms the interests of the inhabitants. Why destroy a valuable economic leverage? The answer: hate, hate, hate.

The Palestinians interpreted the Israeli withdrawal as sign that terror has triumphed, which prompted them to continue. The Palestinian sovereignty turned the Gaza Strip into a terror cell and the inhabitants of the Gaza Strip into hostages of a radical ideology.

Today they talk about lifting the blockade on the Gaza Strip. What does that mean? Is it the removal of the border so that the al-Qaida fighters together with the Hamas fighters could enter Israeli cities with knives, guns, grenades and axes? Will the removal of the naval blockade   lead to the prosperity of the Gaza harbor or to a faster and a more efficient way of unloading heavy weaponry? Is it logical that Israel would allow the entry of a population that wishes to eliminate it?

MAKES NO SENSE!

In this chapter, we saw the "uncompromising yearning of the Palestinians for peace". In the next chapter, we will learn about the "peace process", the process designed to destroy the "despicable Zionist entity".

The peace process

There is nothing like the peace process. From a Western point of view, it represents the chance to pacify the region, to stabilize it and consequently to reduce drastically the instability in the world. From the Palestinians point of view, the peace process is a part of the strategy designed to obtain concessions and gestures, regardless of the terrorism that is carried out simultaneously. Each concession and each gesture brings them nearer to the day when they will try and get the rest by other means.

For clarification purposes, I refer to a recognized program from the 70's known as the "Ten Point Program". [71] Currently it is indeed well camouflaged, but occasionally, in speeches and in forums (not in front of Western audience), it pops up and is referred to as the final objective of the Arab nation and the "Palestinian people" that was created for this purpose.

In this chapter we will survey the peace process and see how it serves the strategic plan of the Palestinians, up to the inevitable confrontation, according to their plan.

As John F. Kennedy once said, for peace to happen:
"Peace does not rest in the charters and covenants alone. It lies in the hearts and minds of all people".

Is this the situation with the Israelis? The answer is yes.

But is this also the situation with the Palestinians? The answer is **No!**

---

[71] More details about the Ten Point Program are available in Wikipedia.

Everybody wants the peace process. The Israelis hope to reach peace, and the Palestinians as part of a strategic plan to achieve as much as possible through diplomacy.

"The Palestinian people" was invented a few generations ago and later on it has formed an identity. This public wishes for a country of its own, contrary to the purpose for which it was established. Just as the United States was a British colony that the British considered as an additional and integral part of them, but eventually a process of separation began and the establishment of a new nation, thus it is expected to happen also with the "Palestinian people". This is perhaps the real chance to establish a homeland for the Palestinian people, but this will not bring the conflict to an end. It will grow stronger. An independent country located a few kilometers away from the major cities of Israel will be able to strategically threat the existence of Israel.

The reason for that is surprisingly simple. As of 2016, there are about 5 million Palestinian "refugees" that are waiting to exercise their Right of Return and return back to the State of Israel. This is what they want. Without that all the rest is purposeless from their point of view.

All along, officials in the Palestinian Authority have declared that they will never recognize Israel as a Jewish state. Abu Mazen, the elected Palestinian leader, does not recognize Israel as a Jewish state, but when a Palestinian state is established he will not allow any Jew to live there. [72] Namely, in the State of Israel millions of Arabs will continue to live enjoying rights equal to those of the Jews, but in the Palestinian state no Jew will be allowed to live. Can you call that peace?

MAKES NO SENSE!

---

[72] More about can be found in http://www.ynetnews.com/articles/0,7340,L-3951626,00.htm

If it were about exchange of population, that is great, it is logical. But what he seeks is the removal of the Jews from the Palestinian state and an Israeli recognition of the refugee problem that they have created with their own hands, as well as populating the small Jewish state with Palestinian population that will constitute a majority in the country.

And even that is not enough, according to him. The "refugees" deserve compensation.

And what about compensating the 1,000,000 Jews who were expelled from Arab countries?

As long as the generation of Palestinians is educated to hate, to self-fulfillment as a martyr and to claiming the entire territory of the State of Israel as their own, peace is not possible.

Remember again: the day Israel puts down its weapon, there will be no Israel, the day the Arabs put down their weapon there will be peace!

Let us try to understand now the "Ten Point Program", and see how it is alive and kicking nowadays.

From Wikipedia [73]: The Ten Point Program of the PLO is the name of the Phased Plan accepted by the Palestinian National Council during its 12th meeting held in June 1974.

---

[73]   Political Program of the 12th Palestinian National Council.

The plan is based on the principles of the policies accepted by the "Palestinian National Council" in the past: the denial of the United Nations Security Council Resolution 242 [74] adopted following the Six Day War, the denial of the existence of the State of Israel, and the demand of the return of all Palestinian refugees to their original homes, [75] and the establishment of an Arab- Palestinian state in the entire region of Palestine (including the territories of the State of Israel). The plan did not establish clear operational steps and did not define any time limits.

The novelty of the PLO in the plan is the pronouncement that any step that will lead to the achievement of these goals is a worthy step. As far as they are concerned, the end justifies the means, and thus to achieve these goals two campaigns have been conducted simultaneously: a diplomatic campaign, aimed to achieve de-legitimization, and a terror campaign.

---

[74] Resolution 242 is a resolution adopted by the UN Security Council after the Six Day War on November 22nd 1967. The purpose of the resolution was to reach a fair and sustainable peace agreement in the Middle East through: 1. Withdrawal of the State of Israel from the territories it occupied in the last war i.e. the Gaza Strip, the Sinai Peninsula, Judea and Samaria and the Golan Heights. 2. Ending the state of belligerency between the State of Israel and its neighbors. 3. Ensuring freedom of sailing in the international sea routes. 4. Finding a fair solution for the refugee problem 5. The establishment of demilitarized zones to ensure the territorial integrity of the countries in the region. 6. The appointment of a UN special envoy for the purpose of maintaining contacts between the countries in the region for the implementation of this resolution.
(From Wikipedia, under the entry: "United Nations Security Council Resolution 242").
[75] Since then the number of refugees has increased from 750,000 to around 5,000,000. Their return to their homes will lead to overcrowding since the number of persons that will return to the same house has increased six times. It is only right that as part of the compensation to the refugees, the State of Israel should expand their homes.

This has created a kind of two camps among the Palestinians. The militant camp, the Hamas, which is located in the Gaza Strip and engages in acts of terrorism and in random rocket launching on cities in the State of Israel. At the opposite side, in the West Bank, the moderate partner is located who is conducting a de-legitimization campaign against the State of Israel and is trying to obtain concessions and gestures by diplomatic means.

Below are two articles from the Ten Point Program:

Article 2 states: [76]
"The Palestinian Liberation Organization will employ all means, and first and foremost armed struggle, to liberate Palestinian territory and to establish the independent combatant national authority for the people over every part of Palestinian territory that is liberated. This will require further changes being effected in the balance of power in favor of our people and their struggle."

Article 4 states:
"Any step taken towards liberation is a step towards the realization of the Liberation Organization`s strategy of establishing the democratic Palestinian State specified in the resolutions of the previous Palestinian National Councils".

This statement leaves no doubt as to the objectives of the Palestinian leadership. The Palestinian territory is the entire territory including the State of Israel and the "occupied territories" (refusal to recognize the UN resolution 242). Article 4 points to the use of the "peace process" as a tactical step that enables to obtain political concessions from the State of Israel, but at the same time not to abandon the process of the armed struggle (terrorism).

---

[76] From Wikipedia under the entry: "PLO`s Ten Point Program".

Article 8 states: "Once it is established, the Palestinian National Authority will strive to achieve a union of the confrontation countries, with the aim of completing the liberation of all Palestinian territory and as a step along the road to comprehensive Arab unity".

The Oslo Accord [77], signed in 1993 between the State of Israel and the "Palestine Liberation Organization", was a serious attempt to solve the ongoing conflict. The Accord was signed on the lawn of the White House with the mediation of US President Bill Clinton. While the State of Israel made sure to follow the articles of the Accord, the Palestinian Authority made sure to breach them with an endless wave of terrorist attacks.

---

[77] In the Oslo Accord, signed on September 13th, 1993 between the late Israeli Prime Minister Yitzhak Rabin and PLO leader Yasser Arafat, mediated by US President Bill Clinton, it was decided on the withdrawal of Israel from the Palestinian towns in Gaza and in the Jericho area, and on the establishment of a Palestinian Authority for an interim period of five years. In the Accord it was agreed to transfer the authority in matters of education, culture, health, welfare, direct taxation and tourism in all the areas of Judea, Samaria and the Gaza Strip to the Palestinian Authority and to set up a Palestinian police force. Then there will be elections to the Palestinian Authority Council. Israel will continue to be responsible for the defense from external threats and will have overall responsibility for the safety of Israelis in these areas. After the interim period a permanent agreement based on the UN Security Council resolutions 242 and 338 will be achieved. The Accord specified that the negotiations on the permanent status will be held not later than three years after the Israeli withdrawal. It also provided that issues such as Jerusalem, Palestinian refugees, Israeli settlements, security arrangements, borders, cooperation with neighbors and other subjects of mutual interest will be part of the   permanent status negotiations.
From Wikipedia under the entry: "Oslo Accord" (Resolutions 242 and 338 deal with ending the hostilities between Israel and its Arab neighbors while finding solutions for the core issue namely, Israeli withdrawal from territories occupied during the six day war, ensuring its security and ensuring the territorial integrity of the countries, finding a just solution to the refugee problem).

From the point of view of Yasser Arafat, Chairman of the Palestinian Authority, signing the Accord corresponded to article 4 of the Phased Plan. Namely, in his opinion, the peace process and terrorism serve the ultimate objective and can coexist.

In an interview to a Radio Monte Carlo radio [78] on September 1st, 1993, after the signing of the Oslo Accord between the PLO and Israel, the Palestinian leader Yasser Arafat said in that the Oslo Accord constitutes the foundation for an independent Palestinian state, according to the principles of the Palestinian National Authority agreed upon in 1974. These principles call for the establishment of a Palestinian National Authority in every part of a Palestinian land that Israel will withdraw from or that will be liberated. [79]

While Israel saw in the Oslo Accord an agreement that will lead to normalization between the Palestinians and the Israelis and will constitute the basis for the establishment of a Palestinian state located next to Israel, Arafat and the Palestinian Authority regarded it as another step in the Phased Plan to achieve everything possible by all means.

---

[78] Radio Monte Carlo includes several radio stations owned and managed by various bodies and is available in several languages such as French, Italian, Arabic, German and Russian.

[79] http://www.palestinefacts.org/pf_1967to1991_plo_phasedplan_1974.php.

Israeli Prime Minister Yitzhak Rabin, PLO leader Yasser Arafat hosted by the United States President Bill Clinton, during the signing of the Oslo Accord ceremony on September 13th, 1993. Vince Musi / The white House.

Bill Clinton, Yitzhak Rabin and Yasser Arafat are photographed during the signing of the Oslo Accord ceremony. The leader of the United States and the Israeli leader are dressed in a suite while Yasser Arafat is still wearing his military uniform.

The Oslo Accord is a repetition of the Hudaybiyyah Treaty, as Yasser Arafat so well said in his speech on May 10th, 1994 in Johannesburg, South Africa:

"I do not consider this Accord of more value than the treaty signed between the Prophet Muhammad and the Quraysh. You remember, the Caliph Umar defied the treaty and referred to it as a deplorable treaty, but Muhammad accepted it, and we are accepting the Accord in the same way". [80]

---

[80] http://counterjihadreport.com/2012/01/15/toxic-taqiyya-satans-greatest-vistory-was-/getting-the-world-to-believe-that-he=did-not-exist

By the Hudaybiyyah Treaty the Prophet Muhammad gained peace with the Quraysh tribe in return for a treaty that humiliated him but allowed him the required time and peace to divert his army to conquer territories. A short time after the signing of the treaty the Prophet Muhammad attacked Jewish Khaybar and subjugated it since Mecca could no longer come to its rescue. In the same way, with the signing of the Oslo Accord the Palestinians received territories, weapons and security men to establish Palestinian Security authorities. From the point of view of Arafat, the enemy helped to equip his soldiers with arms and to train them.

The Hudaybiyyah Treaty was an inspiration for Arafat since it allowed him to quietly get stronger while pretending to seek peace, until the moment he feels strong enough to attack the State of Israel.

Read what he said to ambassadors of the Arab states in a speech he delivered in Stockholm, on January 30th, 1996:

"We the Palestinians will take over everything, including the whole of Jerusalem…..all the rich Jews that will get compensation will go to America…..we in the PLO will focus our main efforts in creating a psychological split in Israeli society by creating two camps. Within five years we are going to be between six to seven millions Arabs in the West Bank and in Jerusalem…..You realize that we intend to eliminate the State of Israel and to establish in its place a pure Palestinian state…….I have no use for the Jews, they have been and they remained Jews. We need all the help we can get from you in the battle for a united Palestine, under an absolute Arab-Muslim rule!" [81]

This is the same Arafat who signed the Oslo Accord to end the conflict while wearing his military uniform. Now you understand why?!

---

[81] http://israeli-arab_conflict.tripod.com/israelandarabs.html

In the end, the ultimate objective according to Arafat is:

"Since we don't have the power to defeat the State of Israel in war, we will do it in phases. We will take every piece of space of Palestine and establish there our sovereignty. We will use this sovereignty as a steppingstone to take more. When the right time comes, we will join with the Arab states for the last battle against Israel. In order to stick to our objective to return to Palestine, we must all grit our teeth sometimes, but this offence must not damage our struggle   against the Zionist enemy……. The rapid withdrawal of Israel from the occupied territories is only the first phase in the establishment of Palestine with Jerusalem as its capital. Only a state like this will be able to continue the battle in purging the enemy from all the Palestinian territories" (November 1994) [82]

As long as the State of Israel cooperates with the "Phrased Plan", no significant difficulties should be expected. Once Israel hesitates, there is also another way that Israel helped, to some extent, to develop which is the supply of weapons, training and an independent territory.

"As long as Israel continues with gestures and concessions, there is no problem. We will continue with the policy of non-violence and peace. But when Israel will say: "That's it, we are not going to discuss Jerusalem, we will not agree to the repatriation of refugees, we are not going to dismantle settlements and we will not withdraw from the borders", all the acts of violence will resume. Only this time we will have 30,000 armed Palestinian soldiers." [83] (Nabil Shaath [84] March 1996, Nablus).

---

[82] http://www.adespicabletruce.org.uk/page24.html

[83] Arafat's War, Efraim Karsh, p.119

[84] Nabil Shaath is a Palestinian politician. He served as Minister for Foreign Affairs in the Palestinian Authority and member in the negotiation team with Israel. From Wikipedia under the entry: "Nabil Shaath".

Even today, Israel is putting out feelers trying to reach an agreement with the Palestinian Authority that controls most of ~~Judea and Samaria~~ the West Bank. With Hamas, located in the Gaza Strip, there is nothing to talk about since it is a terror organization that aims to wipe out the State of Israel.

The Palestinian representative in the Palestinian Authority is Abu Mazen, who used to be Arafat's right-hand man. Abu Mazen said that he has received from the Israeli Prime Minister Ehud Olmert, an even a more generous offer than the one offered by Ehud Barak to Yasser Arafat in Camp David (2000). [85] And yet he did nothing and evaded announcing the end of the conflict and the recognition in a Jewish state.

What`s left to do is to check whether the voice of the people is different from that of its leaders, or as John F. Kennedy said:

"Peace does not rest in the charters and covenants alone. It lies in the hearts and minds of all people".

In all the times Israel negotiated with to the Palestinians, up to the phases when it offered them everything, the Palestinians did not bother to present a counteroffer, but simply said "**NO**" to every offer.

In a negotiation, both parties have to debate, but the situation prevailing now is that Israel makes concessions time after time, while the Palestinians simply say no.

In other words, the Ten Point Program is alive and kicking!

---

[85] http://www.washingtonpost.com/wp-dyn/content/article/2009/05/28/AR2009052803614.html

If you are still skeptical, you should pay attention that the "Palestinian people" is displayed as uprooted, weak and its refugees are scattered everywhere.

If you were part of such people, wouldn`t you be willing to accept an offer to establish a state   on all the "occupied territories" with the blessing of the governments of the world?

What reason would any of you have to refuse, except that you don`t really mean peace?!

Let's check if the people want peace:

The use of facts as a scientific tool that can validate results and estimate them is very common. But when it comes to politics, to hypocrisy, to false hopes, facts are, sometimes, of very little significance, if at all. And then, despite the existence of facts regarding a true reason for the occurrence of events, we sometimes do not allow facts to confuse us. Many people really and truly think (usually without really knowing the actual facts) about the simple intuitive solution.

 For example: who of you knew that a few attempts have already been made in the past to establish a Palestinian state with the encouragement of the State of Israel?

Why did they fail?

More about that, in the next chapter.

Let them have a country already and let`s close the story

We gave, they refused. We insisted, they insisted even more. We begged, they gave us the cold   shoulder. We asked, they answered us down. We prayed, they did not respond to our prayers. Yes, yes, really.

These are the facts, contrary to the propaganda, to the lies and to the demonization of the State of Israel. For example, during September – October 2010 "peace talks" were conducted with the participation of the President of the USA George W. Bush between the Israelis and the Palestinians. This time, as well, nothing was achieved. I bet that also in future peace talks no breakthrough will be achieved.

Why? Because the Israelis do not want peace! You make me laugh, this is a blatant lie, and there is nothing the Israelis want more than peace.

The Palestinians? Oh, they are the victim. Another blatant lie in the endless web of lies.

The problem is not about territory and how much will be left for them and for us, but the very existence of a Jewish state. The Palestinians want everything – the city where I live, the house I live in. They do not see the State of Israel as a legitimate state that was established according to a UN resolution. They consider the tiny State of Israel as an affliction amidst the Islamic nation that has to be removed. The older ones amongst them do not consider themselves as Palestinians, and rightly so, they were molded as a "nation" in 1964, with the establishment of the PLO.

The peace that Israel is so eager to be part of enables them to extort the young country.

In return for a Palestinian acquiescence to talk with the State of Israel, only towards indirect talks, not even towards direct talks, Israel was required to make gestures. One of the gestures included the release of 2,000 prisoners. Not the release of prisoners following negotiations, but the release of 2,000 prisoners in return for starting indirect talks. [86]

The commemoration of the events of the "Naqba" [87] has become an insurmountable impediment to any settlement with the Palestinians. There is a top interest in preserving the "refugee" situation in order to incorporate them in the "peace" agreement, in which Israel will be required (so they hope) to absorb most of them in tiny Israel and give up its existence voluntarily.

The "Gaza Strip" has for long not been "an occupied territory". In 2005 the State of Israel withdrew from the entire territory, but it seems that the territory is indeed occupied by the various terror organizations that have turned it, under Iranian patronage, into a huge arsenal.

The Gaza Strip is a sovereign territory, under the Palestinian responsibility, and they can do with it as they wish. They can build a magnificent infrastructure for the establishment of a Palestinian state, and the money invested in the Gaza Strip is endless.

---

[86] Further details are available in –
http://www.ynetnews.com/articles/0,7340,L-3868430,00.html 26.03.10, Roni Sofer, "Response to US to wait until after Passover".

[87] The "disaster" is a term used for the departure, the flight or the expulsion of about 700,000 Arabs from the Land of Israel during the War of Independence, and their transference to various Arab countries or to other places in Israel, in the West Bank and in the Gaza Strip, thus creating the Palestinian refugee problem, and as a result the demand for the "right of return". From Wikipedia under the entry: "Naqba".

But instead of investing in educating for a better future, in building civil infrastructures, an endless amount is invested headed by Hamas in building nests of terror armed to the teeth, and in setting up al- Qaida bases and all kinds of "seekers of peace". [88]

In the West Bank as well, where over the years a slow acceptance has developed with the fact that this area is intended for the Palestinian "state-to-be", the true identity of this area originally called "Judea and Samaria", names of a distinct Jewish origin, has been blurred (strange, isn't it? occupied territory that has pure Jewish names?).

Just as the Taliban organization makes sure to erase any trace of history that is not Muslim, [89] Muslims all over the world have adopted this method.

Empty churches in Europe become mosques, [90] but does it seem to you possible to turn in Iran or in Saudi Arabia a mosque into a church? Why is it that what they are allowed you are forbidden?

Ancient Jewish territories such as "Judea and Samaria" become over time and sponsored by   propaganda to the "West Bank". This area is administered undisturbed by a Palestinian Authority and the inhabitants enjoy a standard of living and rights unparalleled in the Arab world, except for the Arabs who live within the State of Israel, who enjoy rights arising from the existence of a democracy.

---

[88]   http://news.bbc.co.uk/2/hi/8202553.stm

[89]   http://www.commomdreams.org/headlines01/0301-04.htm
While ignoring an international protest, the Taliban organization destroyed sculptures in the country including two ancient sculptures of Buddha. *March 2001.*

[90]   Paul Belien on Sun, 2006-05-07, "Allah Takes Over catholic Church", http://www.brusseljournal.com/node/1053

The high standard of living [91] that prevails in ~~Judea and Samaria~~ the West Bank, became   possible due to the security fence that separated between the territory of the State of Israel and the "West Bank". The existence of the fence enabled more stability, in addition to the civil and the security infrastructure that the Palestinian Authority succeeded to set up with Israeli, American and European funding [92] (the countries of the "infidels" pour huge amounts of financial aid at a time when they are struggling with one of the worst economic crisis in the world, while the Arab "oil" empires are not keen to help their "oppressed and besieged" bothers – ironic, isn't it?)

Establishing a Palestinian state next to the State of Israel will achieve an opposite effect from what the policymakers of the Islamic Empire hope for. Ending the conflict would be interpreted by them as a failure, because the continued existence of the State of Israel within the area of the Muslim Empire is for them a bitter insult and an affliction that should be removed at all cost.

---

[91]   Bassem Roomie, "The West Bank economy beginning to grow"
http://www.mideastweb.org/west bank economy cg. htm

[92]
http://online.wsj.com/article/SB10001424052748703995104575388754261573556.html "Funding Palestinian Incitement", MATTHEW SINCLAIR AND RAHEEM KASSM

By the way, from the Muslims point of view, every territory that was Muslim and was inhabited by Muslims is a territory that must be returned and is considered by them as an occupied territory. [93] For example: Spain is a territory conquered by the Muslims in 711 and they ruled there until 1492, when the Christians conquered the last Spanish bastion – Granada. According to their doctrine (of the Muslims), patience and demographics will eventually return it to them.

If you still think that the problem is only local then you are welcome to watch the following video that was filmed during the week of the Memorial Day for the 9.11 attacks where a Palestinian Sheikh delivers a special sermon at the "al-Aqsa" mosque that bears a special message for that day to the whole world. The sermon was uploaded onto YouTube [94], so that the sermon of love, of compassion, of brotherhood and of peace is spread forth like wildfire.
"O Allah, a blessed day will come and a sound of prayers will be heard from the roof of the White House to the Red Palace of the Kremlin in Moscow, because Allah gave us the lands of the whole world. O Allah, build already the caliphate and burn them in this world and also in the next". So, the Palestinian Sheik is no longer satisfied with the lands of Palestine, but with the lands of the whole world.

---

[93] From the Hamas Charter, Article 11: "This is the law of Palestine in the Islamic Sharia, this law is the same as the law that applies in any country that the Muslims conquered by force, since during the conquest of the place the Muslims consecrated the countries they have conquered to further generations until Judgment Day arrives" – did you understand that Spain?!

[94] http://www.youtube.com/watch?v=eRuVBsFKXvA
Oh Allah, Blow up the Capitals and Planes of U.S and Russia – Sheikh Muhammad Ayed.

In this part I will bring the facts about the attempts of the State of Israel to grant the Palestinian an independent state. [95]

The first attempt to establish an Arab state in addition to the 22 existing Arab countries was when the United Nations proposed the Partition Plan (November 29th, 1947) that dealt with the partition of Mandatory Palestine into a Jewish state and an Arab state. Note that the resolution does not refer to a "Palestinian state", but to an "Arab state".

The Jews accepted the UN Declaration on the partition of the area into two states with cheers of joy. The Arabs started a war as a response in order to destroy the Zionist entity. The State of Israel that was just born (May 14th 1948) conducted a battle of survival against five Arab countries. Following the ceasefire agreement, ~~Judea and Samaria~~ the West Bank and the Gaza Strip were annexed to Jordan and Egypt respectively. The Arabs were able to establish another Arab country, but Egypt annexed the Gaza Strip and Jordan annexed ~~Judea and Samaria~~ the West Bank.

Remember: at that time there was talk of an "Arab state". The Palestinians popped up in the 60's and were presented as a weak and poor people that was fighting only to get back its historical homeland, with a glorious royal dynasty and an ancient history that dates back to the time when dinosaurs inhabited the globe.

At that time (not of the dinosaurs, but 1948), the Arab population in Israel consisted of a local population and a population that immigrated from the Arab countries in the region following the rise in the standard of living and the need for workers as a result of the development of the Jewish community in Israel.

---

[95] In fact there were 2 additional opportunities – the Peel Commission in 1936-1937 and when the "occupied territories" were annexed for 19 years to Jordan and Egypt.

The second attempt was after the "Six Days War", in 1967.

After the State of Israel`s defeat of the armies of Egypt, Syria and Jordan, the State of Israel believed that was an opportune time to try and strive to end the conflict. The State of Israel offered to give back to Egypt the territories it has occupied in the Sinai and in the Gaza Strip, to the Syrians the Golan Heights and ~~Judea and Samaria~~ the West Bank to Jordan.

The answer was not late to come: a few months later, the Arab League summit was convened in Khartoum, the capital of Sudan, attended by eight Arab heads of state, and at its conclusion the "Khartoum Resolution" was issued (September 1967). The "Khartoum Resolution" contained "Three No`s": [96]

No peace with Israel.
No recognition of Israel
No negotiations with it.
And is short: NO   NO   NO

MAKES NO SENSE!

The State of Israel offered to give back all the territories to those Arabs who crave to-day for a country for their Palestinian brothers. Had the Arabs accepted the offer, the Palestinians, with the blessing of the governments of Egypt and of Jordan, would have already established a state on the territories of the Gaza Strip and ~~Judea and Samaria~~ of the West Bank.

---

[96] Details about this are available on Wikipedia under the entry: "Khartoum Conference".

But what? These territories have been held for 19 years, starting from the War of Independence (1948) until the Six Day War (1967) but no single Palestinian asked for them.

Why? Because there were no Palestinians!

The refusal of the Arabs in the form of the 3 negatives to the Israeli proposal is a most solid evidence about the Arab countries. Imagine living in a country surrounded by enemies whose aim is to destroy your country. Once the attacking armies are defeated, the wining country offers to give back all the territories it has occupied in return for peace. That is all. No compensation for the aggression, not to keep the territories in its possession according to the Laws of War, but only peace. And in return it received 3 times: NO, NO, NO.

The third attempt was at the Camp David Summit, in July 2000.

The Summit was headed by the President of the USA, Bill Clinton, by the Israeli Prime Minister Ehud Barak and by the Chairman of the Palestinian Authority, Yasser Arafat. At the Summit an attempt was made to reach and an agreement that will end the Israeli-Palestinian conflict. The Israeli Prime minister agreed to painful concessions [97], but Yasser Arafat rejected the offers and broke down the peace talks. [98]

---

[97] The concessions included among others: conceding 94% of Judea and Samaria, resettling some of the Palestinian refugees in the State of Israel and finding a comprehensive solution through their resettlement also in neighboring countries, transferring the control in East Jerusalem to the Palestinians and appointing the Palestinians as the guardians of Temple Mount.

[98] The US President, Bill Clinton, blamed Arafat for the failure of the Camp David Summit because he did not compromise in view of the concessions presented by the Israeli Prime Minister, Ehud Barak, and did not offer any counter- proposals.

According to the smiles and the mischief it looks promising! (GPO / Avi Ohayon)

The murderous terrorist attacks by the Palestinians in the form of the Second Intifada, the "Al-Aqsa intifada", resumed after the Summit.

During the Second Intifada over 1,100 Israelis were killed and over 8,000 [99] were injured, mostly by suicide bombers.

John F. Kennedy said:

"Peace does not rest in the charters and covenants alone. It lies in the hearts and minds of all people."

---

[99] See in Wikipedia under the entry: "Al-Aqsa Intifada".

As long as the textbooks portray the Israelis as conquerors,

As long as the Jews and the Israelis are perceived as demonic,

As long as the denial of the Holocaust is taught,

As long as the whole of Palestine is presented as the homeland of the "Palestinian people",

As long as graduation ceremonies include plays in which children martyrs liberate Palestine from the brutal occupation,

As long as the "Protocols of the Elders of Zion" [100] are taught,

As long as there is no education for peace,

There will be no peace between the Palestinians and Israel.

Peace begins in the heart and in the mind, as John F. Kennedy so well expressed it.

Golda Meir, the Prime Minister of Israel, once said regarding the relation of the leadership and of the nation towards their children in the context of turning them into part of the conflict imposed on the State of Israel: "We could forgive the Arabs for killing our children, but we could not forgive them for forcing us to kill their children. Peace with the Arabs will prevail when they will love their children more than they hate us".

---

[100] A reminder: a blood libel that details the malicious Jewish plan to take control over the whole world.

This is a sad reality of leaders who brainwash the minds of the children of the next generation, a new generation of enmity and hate. The Palestinian television broadcasts children programs in which young children are interviewed whose only wish is to get blown up amongst as many Jews as possible, and

A Jew with a devilish look is stuffing himself with an ice cream cone in the shape of al-Aqsa.

virulent propaganda programs present the Jews as cruel conquerors, as monsters who took over Palestine.

How can you make peace with brainwashed people? How it is possible to convince them that reality is different? How can you make peace with leaders who proactively talk about peace, but educate a new generation to violence, to hate and hopelessness?

MAKES NO SENSE!

Each peace initiative encounters a deadlock, but there can be no peace if the Palestinians are not interested in peace but in utilizing the "peace process".

The end of the Camp David process was a cathartic to a process that began a few years earlier. Let's go back to 1993: the Palestinians and Arafat took a unilaterally stance in favor of Saddam Hussein, who occupied Kuwait. While the world has been forming a coalition against Iraq, the Palestinians were practically the only ones who supported Saddam Hussein.

When Iraq launched scud missiles towards population centers in Israel, the Palestinians stood on their roof tops, dancing and rejoicing. A famous song from that period was "Ya Saddam, Ya habib, oodroob, oodroob Tel-Aviv". [101].

It is not the first time that the Palestinians, or the Arabs in the area of Palestine, have chosen the "right side", the "moral side". In the 30's and 40's of the 20th century, the Arabs of Palestine sided with Hitler and with the Nazi regime. To date, the book "Mein Kampf" written by Adolf Hitler is a bestseller in the Muslim world.

The representative of the Arabs in Palestine during the British Mandate, Amin al-Husseini, was known for his opposition to Zionism and for being an avowed anti-Semite.

Al-Husseini was responsible for the terrorist attacks on the Jewish community in the State of Israel during the Arab Revolt and in the beginning of the War of Independence.

His revered figure was Hitler, and he even got to visit him in Nazi Germany.

Al-Husseini established, with the blessing of the Nazi regime, an Arab Unit in Nazi style, "Free Arabia", and he also served in the SS.

---

[101] "Hei Saddam, blow up, blow up Tel-Aviv".

A meeting held between Hajj Amin al-Husseini and Hitler in November 1941. Source: Deutsches Bundesarchiv (German Federal Archive), Heinrich Hoffmann

If someone thinks that something has changed today, he is making a bitter mistake. The Hezbollah, for example, salute by raising the hands, just like in Nazi Germany.

Find the differences:

Hezbollah fighters salute by raising the hands: [(102)]

When the PLO organization and its leader reached the low point following Iraq's loss in the First Gulf War, and their unwavering support in Iraq, Israel rallied in 1993 to help them out by an agreement called "The Oslo Accord".

The Prime Minister of Israel, the late Yitzhak Rabin, with the assistance of members of his cabinet, formulated a new initiative to resolve the conflict in the form of political separation and good neighborly relations. Yasser Arafat utilized the opportunity, and returned from rock bottom to the political arena as the official representative of the Palestinians. The support in Saddam Hussein? All forgiven and forgotten.

[(102)] Hezbollah fighters take an oath to continue the path of resistance against Israel during a Hezbollah parade attended by tens of thousands in a Beirut southern suburb , Friday, December 22, 2000, on the occasion of "Al-Quds Day" (Jerusalem Day)/AP Photo/Hussein Malla)

Both of them met with Bill Clinton, took photos and signed the "Oslo Accord" [103] in September 1993.

Signing the Oslo Accord, 13th of September 1993. The picture shows the President of the USA standing between the Prime Minister of Israel the late Yitzhak Rabin and the Chairman of the Palestinian Authority Yasser Arafat (The Public Library of the USA government).

During the seven years that passed until the convening of the "Camp David Summit" in 2000, the Palestinians have breached every clause in the signed agreement, and all this with the support, the blessing, and the knowledge of Yasser Arafat.

---

[103] The Oslo Accord was signed with the intent to end the conflict between Israel and the Palestinians by a territorial compromise. In the Accord the parties were given mutual recognition in their right to exist (Israel and the PLO).

The suicide attacks, the crime and the corruption increased and Arafat made sure to excite the mass with hate speeches. The Israeli and the Western "commentators" and "leaders" behaved like an ostrich burying its head in the ground, and told the citizens of the country that his speeches were solely in order to protect his position (and if that is indeed the way, what does it say about the will of the "people"?).

In 1994 Yasser Arafat delivered a speech in a mosque in Johannesburg and pointed out among other things:

"This agreement essentially is no more than the agreement signed between our Prophet and a Quraysh tribe". [104]

In the speech, Yasser Arafat compares the Oslo Accord to the Treaty of Hudaybiyyah, a treaty that the Prophet Muhammad signed in 628 AD with members of the Quraysh tribe, with the intent to violate it after he gets stronger.

In 1996 Arafat delivered a speech in Stockholm (the capital of Sweden) in the presence of ambassadors from Arab countries. On that occasion he spoke very clearly to whoever was listening (except for the commentators and the political leaders), and among other things:

"In order to eliminate the State of Israel and establish in its place a pure Palestinian state, we will turn the lives of the Jews intolerable by psychological warfare and overpopulation. Jews do not want to live among us, the Arabs". [105]

---

[104] The full speech is available on: http;//www.textfiles.com/politics/Arafat.txt

[105] The Father of Modern Terrorism. The National Review Online, Andrew C. McCarthy. 22 Sept, 2009.

[106] See in Wikipedia under the entry: "Camp David Summit".

(For some reason, it does not quite seem to me that this is what Yitzhak Rabin signed on with the support of the President of the USA Bill Clinton in the ceremony of signing the Oslo Accord, on September 13th at the White House).

In July 2000 it was agreed to convene the "Camp David Summit", in the holiday residence of the American President. Following the peace agreement that was signed in that place in 1979 between Israel and Egypt, the Americans hoped that with the inspiration of the location   another agreement will be signed, this time between the Palestinians and the Israelis. Israel's proposal included an agreement to establish a Palestinian state on an area of about 94% of ~~Judea and Samaria~~ the West Bank and 100% of the Gaza Strip. [106] Even President Bill Clinton said that Ehud Barak gave the Palestinians everything. [107]

The Palestinians said NO to the proposal and started a timed intifada that claimed the lives of 1,100 Israelis and thousands were wounded.

The fourth attempt was in 2008, when the Israeli Prime Minister Ehud Olmert and the Head of the Palestinian Authority Abu Mazen met.

In an interview to the Washington Post on May 29th, 2009, Abu Mazen detailed an offer he received from the Israeli Prime Minister Ehud Olmert, an offer that was even more generous than the one proposed by his predecessor, Ehud Barak. As always, Abu Mazen declined the offer on the grounds that the "gaps were too large."

---

[106] See in Wikipedia under the entry: Intifada al-Aqsa.

[107] Referring to Mahmoud Abbas, the Chairman of the Palestinian Authority.

What was in the offer? Read the following quote from an article by the journalist Jackson Diehl, and judge for yourself:

"At our meeting on Wednesday, Abbas [108] admitted that Olmert presented to him a map offering a Palestinian state on 97% of the area of the West Bank. He was sorry that the Israeli leader refused to give him a copy of the plan. He confirmed that Olmert accepted the principle of the "right to return" of the Palestinian refugees – something no Israeli Prime Minister has done before. He offered to settle thousands of refugees in the area of the State of Israel. In fact, Olmert's peace initiative was more generous towards the Palestinians than the initiative of Bush or of Bill Clinton. It is difficult to believe that Obama, or an Israeli government, could offer more". [109]

Despite all this, for some reason the Israelis are perceived as peace refusers.

---

[108] Referring to Mahmoud Abbas, the Chairman of the Palestinian Authority.

[109] The Washington Post, Abbas's Waiting Game on Peace with Israel, Jackson Diehl 29th May, 2009 http://www.washingtonpost.com/wp-dyn/content/article/2009/05/28/AR2009052803614.html

Each time the Palestinian rejected the peace offers made by the State of Israel with some pretext, and almost always, before every meeting, Israel made some gestures to the Palestinians, released prisoners, eased the blockade etc.

On the other hand, the Palestinians reward Israel with gestures consisting of shooting attacks, suicide attacks, a few missiles and sometimes even a deadly intifada.

Look again at the size of Israel on the illustration on the right. Notice how ridiculously small the distances are [110] between the center of the Jewish state and the "occupied Palestinian territories". The Israeli Prime Ministers, Ehud Barak in 2000 and Ehud Olmert in 2008, offered more or less all the areas within the borders. In greater Tel-Aviv area live over 3.7 million people who constitute about 40% of the country's population as of 2014. The center of this area is less than 18 km away from the western border of "Judea and Samaria" the West Bank.

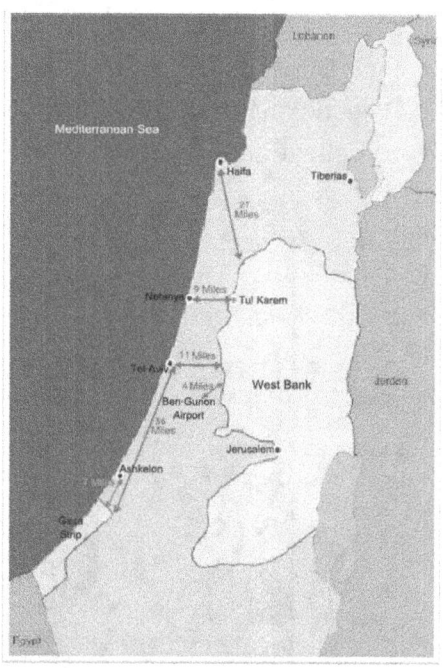

Israel has a bitter taste from the withdrawal attempts in the past. Israel`s withdrawal in 2000 from Lebanon to the international border, was supposed to resolve the conflict with Lebanon.

---

[110] Marked with arrows.

Since then, the Hezbollah organization has settled on the fence and has carried out kidnappings of Israeli soldiers. Following these acts Israel was forced to go to war in order to defend itself.

When Israel made a full withdrawal from the Gaza Strip in 2005, it received in return a cell of terrorism located on its borders launching thousands of rockets and mortar shells toward Israeli cities.

A failure of a peace agreement with the Palestinians can have existential implications for the State of Israel. The distance between the "State Square" in the heart of Tel-Aviv and the border is not more than 18 km. The distance between Israel's international airport and the border is less than 7 km. These are walking distances.

Will anyone think it logical that at a distance of less than 7 km from the JFK airport, a Taliban enclave will be located? Or for example, that the border with the Taliban will cross at a distance of less than 18 km from the center of Paris?

But this, exactly, is the reality the Israelis live in. Luckily, Israel has a strong army to defend it. Had it not been like that, it is most likely that this book would not be written.

See what hatred and propaganda can do: Israel is perceived as a "refuser" of peace, as "stubborn", as an "obstacle" to peace.

The persistent repetition of the lies turns them eventually into a truth, a truth that is almost undisputable. It is imprinted deep in the mind and it changes the subjective reality until it becomes the only truth.

The Arab newspapers are full of disinformation about the intentions of the Israelis. The demonization and the exaggeration turn the Jews and the Israelis

From an Arab newspaper

111

into evil plotting monsters and into cruel, bloodthirsty soldiers. Anti-Semitic cartoons that show the Jews in a light reminiscent of a dark period, are distributed constantly and uninterruptedly.

See as an example a cartoon depicting the Jews as warmongers that drown the peace-loving Arabs in a sea of blood. Think what a picture like that does deep in the subconscious. How it combines with the incessant brain washing and becomes part of the "pure truth", which is one big fabrication.

This state of mind is not shared by the Palestinians, the Arabs or the Muslims only, but it has become universal.

For example, an interview published on the Ynet website with the French movie actor Vincent Lindon on 14.06.2010. During the interview, there was also talk about peace and about the stubborn refusal of the Israelis to make peace in the face of the outstretched hand for peace of the Palestinians, the hand that is holding the olive branches.

In the words of the interviewee: "Excuse me, but when the hell are you planning to wake up and finally make peace with the Palestinians? You don`t understand that one day, sooner than you think, the world will be fed up with the Israelis? Isn`t it clear that very soon people will say to themselves: 'Wait a minute, there are seven million Jews driving the world crazy against 200 million Arabs all around who are a wonderful potential for business. Let these Jews go to hell!' This is going to happen and this says to you a Jew whose grandfather was Head of the Jewish National Fund. How long do you think you can still hold on before the whole world will be fed up with you? It is skilling me. People are unable to make a move and head a self-evident change". [111]

When the endless propaganda machine is changing reality according to its needs, when there is readiness, based on prejudice, to accept that fictional reality, it is easy for a lie to bury the truth, and many believe that making peace depends only on the State of Israel, while ignoring in fact that the "peace negotiation" is headed by a Doctor for Holocaust denial, [112] and in section 15 of the Palestinian Charter which was supposed to be nullified, but was never canceled, it is written: "Liberating Palestine, from an Arab viewpoint, is a national duty, in order to ward off from the big Arab homeland the Zionist and the imperialist invasion and purge Palestine from the Zionist existence". [113]

Moreover, the Hamas Charter opens with the following words: "Israel will continue to exist until Islam wipes it out, as it has wiped out others before it......" [114]

---

[111] Merav Yudilovitz, "Eventually the world will be fed up with the Israelis", http://www.ynet.co.il/articles/1,7340,L3904546,00.html

[112] In 1982 Mahmoud Abbas got his PhD in history in the Soviet Union at the Lumumba University. His thesis dealt with "The connections between Nazism and Zionism in the years 1933-1945", which included motifs of Holocaust denial: among other things it referred to the opinion of those who reckon that the number of those killed during the Holocaust was much smaller than the accepted one – from Wikipedia under the entry: Abu Mazen.

[113] From Wikipedia under the entry: "Palestinian National Charter".

[114] THE COVENANT OF THE HAMAS.

And despite all these evidences, the endless propaganda manages to turn the tables: Israel and its inhabitants are barbarians, warmongers who put the idea of peace to ridicule.

These slanders convince not only marginal newspapers, but also newspapers that are considered (at least in their own eyes) as "respectable".

The "Time" magazine, [115] for instance, stated that the Israelis are indifferent. A photographer on its behalf took pictures of three young men who were sitting on the beach smoking a Narghile. The reporter quoted a real estate agent who said that he was selling apartments also when Qassams rockets were falling down, and in order to conclude the thesis imprinted already deep in his blurred and biased mind, the reported inserted in the article findings of a survey that "proved" that only 8% of the Israelis consider the conflict with the Palestinians as a problem.

And why? Because most of the issues that have been bothering the Israelis were connected with the situation of education and with national security. In fact, interviewees describe an attempt to conduct a normative life routine even under difficult conditions. It is worth mentioning that during World War II, during the German "Blitz" on London, the British tried to conduct a normal life routine. They went about their business despite and in spite the constant threat on them, and this behavior was a source of national pride.

A simple analysis of the article will show that at first sight it seems like an innocent article, but in fact it conceals a distinct narrative that presents the Israelis as the "bad party" in the story. Thus, each failure is automatically perceived as Israel's failure and its exclusive responsibility.

---

[115] The full article is available in:
http://www.time.com/time/magazine/article/0,9171,2015789,00.html

Something to think about: every now and then there are discussions about advancing the establishment of a Palestinian state in the territories of ~~Judea and Samaria~~ the West Bank, in a route bypassing Israel, i.e., a unilateral proclamation of a state with east Jerusalem as its capital. Do you think that if that in fact happens there will be peace and at long last the conflict will come to an end? You make me laugh!

If a Palestinian state is established, the pressure will be directed to turning Israel within the green line to a citizenship-based state, and later on – to another Arab country in the Middle East.

This book is part of a series of books I have written about the Middle East. I made sure to write the books so that they fully exhaust the subject, are informative, and free of political correctness so that they will actually present facts and truths concerning the conflict in the Middle East with the aim to show a different angle from the one that the media and many activists show out of an agenda and worldview that ignore facts and historical truths. I hope you will find this book and other books that I have written useful and eye openers that cast a different light on the reality in the Middle East. As a writer, I would be happy to get a positive review in the book website from which this book was purchased because it would help me, with your generous help, to spread the truth to other readers who are eager to learn more about the conflict that is taking place in the Middle East.

In order to enhance the understanding of the Middle East I welcome you to deepen reading the book series I have written on this subject called: "Understanding the Middle East".

The books are available through an assigned website: www.kobisha.com

Or type "Kobi Shashoua" in the Amazon website.

You are welcome to contact me directly by e-mail: kobimnsil@gmail.com

And by phone: 972-54-8030648

Yours Truly,

Kobi Shashoua